Four Poets on Poetry

Four Poets

on

Poetry

EDITED AND WITH

AN INTRODUCTION BY

Don Cameron Allen

THE JOHNS HOPKINS PRESS: BALTIMORE

The Percy Graeme Turnbull Lectures

In November, 1958, The Johns Hopkins Poetry Festival was held in Baltimore. The program consisted of readings and lectures by eight of America's foremost poets: Archibald MacLeish, Yvor Winters, Marianne Moore, John Crowe Ransom, E. E. Cummings, Robert Frost, R. P. Blackmur, and Mark Van Doren. The lecture part of the Festival—by R. P. Blackmur, Yvor Winters, Marianne Moore, and Mark Van Doren—was sponsored by the Percy Graeme Turnbull Lecture Committee as the regular biennial Turnbull Lectures, organized and directed by Don Cameron Allen, of The Johns Hopkins Department of English.

The four essays, introduced and edited by Don Cameron Allen, are presented in this book so that they may be read and enjoyed by a larger audience than could attend the Festival.

Contents

Don Cameron Allen   1   Introduction

R. P. Blackmur   24   Edwin Muir: between the Tiger's Paws

Yvor Winters   44   Poetic Styles, Old and New

Marianne Moore   76   Dame Edith Sitwell

Mark Van Doren   83   The Poems of Thomas Hardy

109   Index

Four Poets on Poetry

Don Cameron Allen

Introduction

IN ITS BRIGHTER AND HIGHER aspects the purpose of all human thinking is the capture of a greatly desired but agilely elusive substance called truth. The nature of this substance, or perhaps it is only a quality, is grievous to define, and for this reason its pursuit is difficult. Philosophers, on whom we depend for our knowledge of abstractions, have exerted themselves beyond measure to lock whatever they have felt or half-known about truth into the steel cell of a comprehensive and endurable statement. Sometimes they will say that truth is the apparent correspondence of an intellectual proposition to reality; sometimes they will say just the opposite. Theologians tell us that truth is a matter of revelation, but empiricists inform us, then, that there is no implement labeled revelation in the cabinet of knowledge.

In a more honest and less complex age than ours, truth was often measured by the *consensus gentium*. Whatever was accepted by the majority of peoples in most places through a great deal of time was assumed to be true. This was a good doctrine for men of more naïve but happier generations, but more than three hundred years ago it began to lose respect. The genial Montaigne, who lived during the sixteenth century, was shocked to discover how different and contradictory were human notions about matters that cultivated Europeans thought innately understood. In the centuries since Montaigne's death the situation has not improved; nevertheless, there is something in the heart of man that impels him to seek the face of truth although it is likely to be a face veiled or distorted by grimace. Hence, though we cannot define truth, we pursue it; and though the quarry is very much like a phantom fox fleeing through a foggy meadow, we have, good huntsmen that we are, attempted to establish some rules of the chase. We know the laws of the field and the forest even though we do not know what we hunt.

In the same age in which Montaigne was weaving the fabric of doubt and urging men to try truth by the paradox, Sir Philip Sidney took up the challenge of the anti-poets—the challenge invented by the poet Plato—and attempted to defend poetry as a form of thinking and a means to truth. He had the good sense to base his *Apologie for Poetrie* on supra-empirical arguments and to select his best weapons from the armory of the anti-poets. What he wrote was actually a lawyer's brief, and he opens his case by pleading that poetry requires no defense because it is all a matter of taste. It is something we like or dislike, and nothing can really be done about it. But having spoken as an advocate with full attention to the rites of forensic practice, he concludes, when he has reached the tail of his defense, as a theologian, inviting us to believe in revelation.

> *Believe* that [poets] were the first bringers-in of all civility . . . *believe* . . . that no philosopher's precepts can sooner make you honest than the reading of Vergil; . . . *believe* . . . that it pleased the Heavenly Deity . . . under the veil of

fables to give us all knowledge, logic, rhetoric, philosophy, natural and moral, and *quid non*; . . . *believe* . . . that there are many mysteries contained in poetry, which of purpose were written darkly lest by profane wits it should be abused; . . . *believe* that they are so beloved of the gods that whatsoever they write proceeds of a divine fury.

For Sidney, as for some critics and poets who succeeded him, poetry is a kind of religion. He would probably have said that an anti-poet could not be a religious man. He also realized that poetry must be believed tantamount to revelation, and he held for this reason that it was superior as a mode of thought and a form of knowledge to both history and philosophy. I should hardly want to go so far as Sidney and set up an evaluative hierarchy because such an attempt would be not only perilous but, in this late age, vain. However, the poet of *Astrophel and Stella* has made a pattern for me; and after adding science and scientific thinking to his list of intellectual disciplines, I should like eventually to consider poetry as a means of thought and as a repository of knowledge.

When Thucydides, the father of history, sat down to write his account of the Peloponnesian War, he was so conscious of the novelty of the undertaking that he felt called upon to explain what he was doing. "My conclusions," he said, "are drawn from proofs that may safely be relied on. Assuredly they will not be disturbed either by the lays of a poet displaying the exaggerations of his craft, or by the compositions of chroniclers whose main attraction is their avoidance of truth." There is no question about what is said here. A good historian is a diligent scanner of the appearances of reality who avoids the entanglements of the imagination as incompatible with the due processes of reason. Thucydides and his lineal descendants have generally contented themselves with reporting the facts in spatial contexts and chronological sequences that are agreeable to the unimaginative section of the brain. "If I have used a fine style," says the historian Cassius Dio, fearful that his readers would think him a man of letters, "no one on this account will, I hope, question the truth of the narrative; for I have endeavoured to be exact . . . as far as possible." This fear of literary taint is consonant with the injunctions of Thucydides, and we can well imagine the chagrin of a modern historian whose book was described as "fanciful."

History may certainly be a treasury of knowledge, but the historian thinks by assembling without exaggeration or ornamentation a sequence of dead facts that resemble truth in the past tense. The basic difference between history and poetry or the historian and the poet, as the Greeks made it out, is found in Lucian's *The Way to Write History*. This amiable Syrian of the second century cannot endure what he calls "word painting," and he abominates historians who describe events that never occurred. These types of writing, he complains, are the common habits of poets "although one has always thought that there was some difference between the two arts." I suppose that if we want history, Lucian is right. What we ask of an historian is an accurate account of what happened, or what, according to most witnesses, seemed to happen. If the historian was present at a battle, a coronation, an election, a treaty of peace, or a pact of alliance, we hope that he has made allowance for his personal excitement or psychic state, for the sort of season and time of year, for the smoke of cannon or of oratory, for noise, confusion, point of vantage, and the bad correction in the left lens of his eye-glasses. If he works with documents, as most historians do, we hope that he has evaluated their genuineness, searched out the prejudices of their authors, and smoothed out their distortions. We also trust that he has been able to separate the almost true from the slightly false. The poet, who is attempting our imagination and through it our feelings, who will convince us by metaphor rather than by syllogism, will happily violate all of the historians' rules. He will twist and expand the evidence; he will embrace the testimony of the least reliable and most imaginative witnesses; he will, as Lucian says in his lament over the fanciful historians, "have one man kill seventy at a blow." For the poet is committed by his metaphor to enlargement just as the historian is urged to containment by the fact.

Examples of the distortion of the historical doctrine by poets may be observed whenever a poet selects an historical theme as the subject of his imaginative meditations. When, for instance, Shakespeare wrote *King Lear*, he turned for his preliminary information to a firmly trusted book, the *Histories of the Kings of Britain* by Geoffrey of Monmouth. Here he read of the foolish old king, who had three daughters of whom he loved Cordelia, the youngest, the best. Resolving to divide his kingdom, he proposed a love test in which Cordelia fared badly, but not so badly that she was unacceptable as a dowerless bride to the king of France. Then Lear is treated harshly by the other daughters, flies to France, and is restored by Cordelia's armies to his throne. He rules bravely for three years, dies, and his beloved Cordelia, now a widow, succeeds him. The end is bitter. The sons of the evil sisters rebel; Cordelia is defeated and imprisoned, "wherein," says Geoffrey, "overwhelmed with grief of her lost kingdom, she slew herself." This is the story retold by the British historians and put in rime by some of Shakespeare's lesser contemporaries. The end is always the same;

and for most men of the Elizabethan age, the damp of gloom rises not from the sufferings of Lear, but from the despair and suicide of Cordelia. It is the historically accurate but unendurable climax; it violates all the emotions. We ask ourselves, as Shakespeare must have asked himself, whether the life of a charming and devoted young woman, who had rescued her misjudging father, should end in self-destruction.

It is small wonder that Shakespeare was repelled by this history, for it makes all things awry and fouls his poetic definition of the universe. It was unseemly to him that a girl, benevolent and forgiving, should yield to the sin of despair, the sin against the Holy Spirit. Granted that all of this happened in pre-Christian Britain, the end was too savage; for even the wild gods of Euripides see to it that the pious and devoted Iphigenia is preserved. It was unbelievable that Cordelia should be found in that circle of Hell where suicides are suspended "each on the thorny tree of its tormented shade." So Shakespeare turns his back on history and makes a minority report. The battle is lost; Lear never regains the crown; and Cordelia is murdered in prison by the forces of evil against which Shakespeare eternally protests. It is a new end to history that Lear himself foresees.

> Upon such sacrifices my Cordelia
> The gods themselves throw incense.

Despair finds no port or entry in the character of Cordelia as Shakespeare remade her. She is cleansed of her historical disease, and it is transferred instead to her father and to his alter ego, the Duke of Gloucester. From the emendable despair of these two men, the theme of Shakespeare's tragedy is wrought. By concentrating on the eating desperation and anger of Lear,

Shakespeare denies the testimony of the historians and invents a new rule by means of which the character of Lear may be construed. The histories say little about this. The king, says Geoffrey, was "grieved beyond measure," and this moderate statement is not inflated by Geoffrey's successors. Even in the anonymous play of *King Leir*, which is Shakespeare's partial model, the despair and remorse of Lear is so tame that we are totally unaffected. Yet it is from this germ of suggestion that Shakespeare, thinking as a poet, begets the titanic passion, the brain-rending misery that besets the aged king. To call forth this passion and this misery, he creates a man whom the historians have never known.

When I observe that poetry and poetical thinking have almost nothing in common with history and historical thinking, I expect that some critics of literature and some historians will agree with me. I am also aware that historians are still urged to use literary texts as documents, which, indeed, they never are; and that some critics will always be busy with the historical background of literature, which is a pleasant but generally unattractive form of non-literary effort. But this type of self-entertainment is probably not so wasteful as that of those critics who hold that poetical thinking is a half-sister to scientific thinking and that poetry is a kind of science. In this age when the sciences have been inclined to adopt in certain of their areas a quasi-imaginative character, this form of speculation is likely to carry a little weight.

The poet, say the proponents of the science of poetry, is as fascinated as the scientist by the inner nature of things and never concerns himself, as the historian does, with external appearances. This is Wordsworth listening to the systole and diastole of nature; this is Browning seated, notebook in hand, at humanity's couch; this is even Milton connected by some sort of fleshly short wave to the council halls of Heaven and Hell. The critics of literature who are dazzled by this illusion are aided and abetted by the agitated outcries of certain theoretical scientists who are engaged in establishing an electronic proof of the existence of God. The fault that mars this hypothesis is that it is neither scientific nor poetic, since it depends on a sort of uncontrolled imagination that is inimical to both science and poetry.

I should be the first to admit that there is some sort of connection between the engendering idea of the poet and what used to be called the "scientific hunch," but it is exactly at this point that all similarities between science and poetry cease. Bitter as the realization may be, we must remember that philosophers—those men who are mainly concerned with areas of knowledge abandoned by the scientists, theologians, psychologists, economists, political theorists, and aestheticians—long ago gave up the search for what was once called inner essence or the-thing-in-itself. When philosophers withdraw from any proposition, it has to be totally impossible as a subject of speculation. No scientist, I think, is likely to assume that there is a difference between appearance and reality; and we can hardly believe that what the scientist has thrown over as a reasonable subject of inquiry, the poet through some special endowment has fruitfully discovered.

In the main, science and poetry, scientific and poetical thinking have almost nothing in common. The scientist is really engaged in averaging external experience into laws. The poet, on the contrary, is ordinarily unimpressed by the average and is principally attracted by uniqueness, by the sort of phenomenon that the scientist calls the variant, the aberration of a fixed order.

But the scientist and the poet are separate in other respects. The scientist is eager, I think, to convey his impressions of the average of appearances in the linguistic cart of non-subjective symbols that will be recognized by his fellow scientists, who will answer him in the same symbols. The poet is not averse to symbols; he is, in fact, trapped by them into his poem; but his notion of symbols is entirely different from that of the scientist. The scientist wants an unambiguous symbol that will mean exactly the same thing to all other scientists. The poet, too, wants his symbols to have meaning, but his are not limited meanings. The poem of his youth may have even for him a different meaning in old age. For his readers—and I am thinking of the informed and sensitive ones—it may have still other meanings. Accuracy is not an end for the poet, and it is not guaranteed by the modes of poetical thought. But there is another difference between the symbolic language of the poet and that of the scientist.

For the scientist the symbol is a means of conveying fact; for the poet it is a way of transmitting emotion. This emotion has no connection with hysteria or with nervous agitation. It is plainly the emotion attendant on a creative act carried through or on the uniqueness of the metaphor that releases the poet from further speculation. Its validity comes from success or relief and sometimes from both. It is at each end of its circuit completely subjective, and in this major respect it is altogether unscientific. A scientist who wishes to tell another scientist about a stone will probably say that it is " a concreted earthy or mineral substance of such-and-such chemical composition." A poet will drop the same stone in a forest pool and describe it with the birdsong evoked by the splash of the water. What the bird sings will tell the poet's readers, as it has told him, all that need be known about the stone, the pool, and the forest. But this is certainly not science, and it is not the way the scientist thinks.

If poetry is not history or science, if the way the poet thinks is not like the way the scientist or the historian think, we may ask ourselves whether or not we find some connection between poetry and philosophy or the poet and the philosopher. Sidney saw a connection, but he thought that the poet's thought was better thought. The poet and the metaphysician share the analogical process, and both poets and philosophers stand outside the material engagements of modern life in a way that is different from the disengagements of the historian and the scientist. When we turn through histories of literature, we come on men who are described as "philosophic poets," although we never find in the histories of philosophy the mention of a "poetical philosopher." The denomination of "philosophical poet" is probably unfortunate; but we have persisted in this unhappy contradiction, and we even write books called *The Philosophy of Milton* or Shakespeare or Shelley when really we mean something else. We are, I suppose, inclined to believe as the ancients were that *poet, prophet,* and *philosopher* are synonyms.

The father of philosophy is reported to have said that no sane man knocks on the door of poetry and to have banished poets from his republic; yet Plato, as defenders of poetry have tirelessly pointed out, was something of a poet himself. Then, too, when we read the remains of the philosophers before Socrates we often find expressions that seem to be poetic rather than philosophic. "Nature," writes Heraclitus, "likes to hide." "Victory," says Democritus, "betrays the survivors." Empedocles appears to have the poetical manner when he says, "Stepping from summit to summit, not to travel one path of words to the end," or "the air sank down on the earth with its long roots." This is all usable poetic stuff, but the question does not rest here. Is it philosophy?

If I can assume that prior to Aristotle, philosophers not only thought like poets but were poets, I can be equally sure that since that age they have lost their poetic touch. I am quite ready to agree that there are poetic moments in Bruno, Fichte, and Schopenhauer; Santayana is the most poetical of philosophers and, perhaps, the most philosophical of poets. This is all true, but I also notice that philosophers are most poetical when they are least philosophical. We have, for instance, a fragment of Empedocles which reads, "draining their lives with bronze." Now this may have something to do with the war before Troy, but it might also refer to Greek materialists who were spending themselves in hopes of amassing a fortune. In either case the image is neat and suggestive, and no poet would reject it, but I do not believe that it would gain admittance to the *Journal of Philosophy* in its Empedoclean shape. It would have to be revised to read something like this: "The current inclination towards the dissipation of the life force in the temporality of material contention is one of the principal amoral stimuli of this century." The difference in the two statements is obvious. Empedocles is more stirring, unliteral, non-exact. As in the case of scientific thinking, it is again a question of univalence versus multivalence, or rational thought versus imaginative thought.

In the history of so-called philosophical poetry, only Lucretius and Dante have been eminently successful as poets. Lucretius, who has a mild enough philosophical success to be mentioned in histories of that art, is, as any Latinist knows, a far better poet when he is composing a hymn to Venus or standing in artistic awe before the circle of the stars than when he is mirroring

Epicurus and discussing the *clinamen* of the atoms. Dante succeeds as a philosophical poet because he is not a philosophical poet at all. Had he put the *Summa Theologica* into *terza rima*, he would be unread and probably unknown except to professional mediaevalists. He excels and has his place in the forum of poetry because he exemplified the doctrines of Aquinas; he does not describe or expound them. We understand Dante's aesthetic better if we have read Aquinas; we do not read Dante to comprehend the *Summa*.

Poets are seldom philosophers, and they do not get sealed of this tribe by carrying a philosophical system into verse. Some poets of second- or third-class talent have attempted this metamorphosis into philosopher with no success, which is a way of saying no art. They were the victims, I suppose, of the ancient fallacy that whatever is true is beautiful and that whatever is beautiful is poetic; so they confused poetic truth with philosophic truth without realizing that they had naught in common. A sound philosophical system can never be made poetry by hanging it over with metaphors; abstraction has a quiet beauty of its own but it is not that of poetry. Actually, an idea has poetic value only when it is born in poetic shape. The shape and the idea are inseparable; they cannot be forced on each other.

But philosophy used to concern itself with human conduct, with ethics and morality, and there are still some critics left who like to argue that poetry joins with philosophy in cogitating these matters. They are not so naïve as the old-fashioned explicators who sought for the " moral " in the poem. Now they talk about social criticism and human integration which puts it all on a much higher platform, but the end is about the same. As a consequence of this, I must ask myself whether poetry, since it is unconcerned with what is philosophically true, is really engaged in considering what is ethically good. Most philosophers would agree that what they call justice, fidelity, temperance, liberality, and fortitude are ideal ethical goods which all reasonable men should search out. The opposites of these notions, they would certainly say, should be avoided by social, even by solitary, man. But if poets agreed with this, we should be wanting some rather fine poetry. Out of intemperance, Shakespeare made Falstaff; out of infidelity, Macbeth; out of illiberality, Shylock; out of injustice, Othello. I shall not say that Shakespeare approved of viciousness, for the contrary is clearly the truth; but evil played an immense role in his poetical thinking, and it has often been the point of suggestion for other poets as well. It goes without question that poetry can be made out of material that lacks the stamp of ethical approval. Moral ugliness and physical ugliness can both be transformed into intense artistic attractiveness. A fascinating study could be made, I expect, of the aesthetic of ugliness just as studies were long ago made about the morality of immorality.

It must be clear by now that I do not think that philosophical thinking is like poetical thinking or that philosophy has a firm engagement with poetry. Poetical thought feeds on metaphors. They are its heart and center. For history, philosophy, and science they are dubious adjuncts. Somehow or other the essential difference between these forms of knowledge is here. Granted that all of these means of truth-seeking share in each other's rights and sometimes are woven loosely together, the poetical process of thought seems to me to be more different from the others than they are among themselves. Euclid alone may have " looked on beauty bare "; and I should be the last to question the poetic possibilities of geometry, or the philosophical experience of reading Milton, or the historical values of the *Iliad*; nonetheless, merely to say this suggests, however, that the dissimilarities between these forms of thought are greater than their dependencies. But if poetical thinking is different and if poetry is wisdom, how do we understand this thought and know this wisdom?

In antiquity it was doubted whether poets thought at all. The *Odyssey* begins with "Tell me, O Muse," and many of the older Greek poets announce that they have been presented with their verse by one or other of the fair, bare ladies who haunt the Castalian springs. The first of the English poets, Caedmon, was said to have been so forlorn of poetry that he left the hall where men were singing in tune to the harp and retreated to the byre where the cattle would not ask him for a song. There an angel, the natural Christian Muse, came to him and told him to sing, inspiring him with the topics of his song, and thus he became the first poet of the Angles and Saxons. This elder notion that the poet is the trumpet of the will of God, a notion that Donne emphasizes in *The Second Anniversary*,

> The purpose and th' authoritie is his;
> Thou art the Proclamation; and I am
> The Trumpet, at whose voyce the people came,

persists even unto this day among primitive peoples. The shaman or seer who recites at tribal functions is thought to be the receptacle of a mysterious power that fills him with its words. He is a sort of savage Milton, who can tell confidently

> Of my Celestial Patroness, who deignes
> Her nightly visitation unimplor'd,
> And dictates to me slumbering, or inspires
> Easie my unpremeditated verse.

The inclination to invoke the Muse or the Holy Spirit gave way during the latter part of the eighteenth century to a tendency on the poet's part to invoke himself. It is only occasionally that a later poet—Hopkins for instance—will admit that his poetry "is given him." There is, I think, in this notion that poetry is intelligential rather than ratiocinative, a partial key to the nature of poetical thought.

Schiller once defined art as a form of play, and Vico, the precursor of the critic Croce, said that poetry is the language of children. Some time ago Auden was asked by someone who ought to have known better why poets wrote poetry. To this absurd question he offered a wise answer: they wrote poetry because it was fun. The word that he used is a word that children have always in their mouths. Now I do not think that Schiller or Vico or Auden would say that poetical thinking is childish and that it is improper for adults to write poetry. What all of these men meant is that poetical thinking is totally different from all other kinds of thinking, and that maybe the child's way of observing the universe and describing it is something like the poet's way. There are, I believe, no child philosophers, although Wordsworth knew some, and this fact gives us Wordsworth's definition of philosophy. I can think of no child historians, and the child scientists I have encountered are more child than scientist. But in some degree, in love of rime and of metaphor, the child makes common ground with the poet. The child's way of seeing his world—uncluttered by adult experience, pretensions, and customary patterns of observation—is similar in its uniqueness and surprise to the way that poets see and record experience.

The English poet Traherne, who drew much of his poetical thought from the recollections of his childhood, comes close to the explanation of this notion of the child's world and the poet's world in several of his poems. It is a world in which there is no difference between *me* and *you*, no boundary between the real and the imaginary, between sleep and waking, between poetical thinking and logical thinking. But it is a world that is lost as maturity teaches distinctions.

> O that my Sight had ever simple been!
> And never faln into a grosser state!
> Then might I evry Object still have seen
>   (As now I see a golden Plate)
> In such an hev'nly Light, as to descry
> In it, or by it, my Felicity.

Traherne had to grow up to say this because in the world of his childhood there could be no poetical thinking. In that world all was poetical. The distinctions between the real and the imaginary, between dreaming and waking, have to be made before poetical thinking can come to being. Perhaps this discrimination does not exist; perhaps in stating it I am guilty of a childlike error; nonetheless, it seems to me that there are no dreams in a world of dreams and no poetry where all is poetry. Alexander Pope is saying something like this when he remarks "that he did not wander in fancy's mazes long / But stoop'd to truth and moralized his song." He knew a frontier when he crossed it. The state of fancy was of a different geographical color for him than the realm of philosophical ethics. By making this distinction he was a poet.

Poetical thinking is dependent on logical thinking for the establishment of these lines of demarcation, but in no other respects is it like logical thought. Poetical thinking makes its own rules according to the temperament and skill of each thinker; it abounds in syllogisms that a logician would call false. On the other hand, the historian, philosopher, and scientist follow fixed modes of thought and dominate the appearances of reality by set logical formulae. When it comes to keeping the law, the true poet is an outlaw. There are no rules that we can master that will make us poets, or if we are poor poets, better poets. We may read poetry incessantly. As so many Aristotles, we may tabulate the methods of poets, compile treatises on metrics, structure, rime, and imagery. We may talk about texture and paradox, tenor and vehicle. We may get all of these discoveries by heart, but none of us will be poets because of it. For all of his effort, Aristotle never got to the heart of Greek poetry let alone making himself or his readers the peers of Homer or Euripides. The reason for all of this ill-success is that, unlike logical thinkers, poets work with material that no man can overcome. They may plan a poem in detailed fashion. They may even work out those carefully reasoned structures that scholars and critics are always finding in poems. But if they cannot illogically discard their plan and break their preconceived structure, they are not poets.

A poet constantly astonishes himself, I think, by violating the rules of logical thought. When I say this, I, as a non-poetical thinker, am leaning on the few facts that I have—the working manuscripts of poets. The thinking poet does not walk down the finely swept path of a formally developed and sequent series of logical postulates. He advances by metaphor, which is a form of leaping. The philosopher, the historian, the scientist move as snails on a slate and leave behind them a glistening trail that we can follow with even an unpracticed eye. The poet moves like a ground squirrel; where he is now gives no promise or assurance of where he will be next. He writes a line. He emends it or strikes it out. He makes additions. He switches terms. He throws a stanza away. We can follow him for a moment. We can sometimes explain a change or a sequence by semantics or allusion or association. Then he expunges and achieves the final, the successful version. Often this version has small connection with the earlier tentations.

So, in a sense, poetical thinking can no more be explained than a poem can be explained. Socrates, we remember, complains on one occasion that poets never answer the question, " What does this poem mean? " Rhetoricians, grammarians, pedants, poetical parasites, as he suggests, are always ready to write explanations of poetry. In this observation history bears him out. The great Greek poets who followed Homer do him the honor of borrowing a fable, a phrase, a metaphor, as if to say, " No one else could do this better." It is not until the time of Pindar that he is mentioned at all, and then the simple expression " his divine epics " is enough. Late in the history of classical letters, a second-class poet, Manilius, makes more of him.

> Greece does not know his country,
> Yet there flowed from him
> A singing river for all later men
> Rich in the goods of one man.

While the poets stood in modest silence before the poet, the non-poets—Theagenes of Rhegium, Metrodorus of Lampsacus, Eustathius, Apollonius Dyscolus, Aristarchus, and many others— were correcting, explaining, understanding. If Homer had lived to have read them, he would have thanked his blindness.

Though poetical thinking is essentially non-logical, and though in its way it is detached from common reality, it is not opposed to reality. There is a division between them, not a difference. The poetical mind is separated from reality only in those moments when it is thinking poetically, in those moments when for it the imaginary is the real or the real the imaginary. The poet stands outside of the real in his imagination, but he brings the real into a contracted kind of individual existence through the metaphor that fantasy awards him. The reality of the metaphor can be tested only against other metaphors, and the test is made certain by the intensity of emotional acquiescence. The critic— and by that word I mean the logical thinker in the common sense—is seldom capable of this experience. If he is a non-poet, as he often is, he would consider it mental confusion, a kind of controlled schizothymia. He is always able to sever and to keep totally separate the reason and the imagination, the real and the imagined. For this reason, critics are sometimes taunted with being frustrated poets, but as a matter of fact every completely logical man or simply every man who tries to think logically is a frustrated poet. In the same manner the poet, who can obviously live for only a fraction of each day in the realm of the imagination, who can think poetically at only isolated and discrete moments, is a frustrated child. The logician might conclude that the poet lives an imperfect life because he occupies two planes of thought and is, consequently, two different men. I cannot deny the logician's right to say this, but it also seems to me that the poet's relations with what we call reality may be more complete than those of all other men.

The real is not real to the poet because it is real; it is real because it is fitting. Poets have always talked about seeing things as they are, and in earlier times they held mirrors up to nature and wrote down what was therein reflected. The problem in these statements is linguistic. *Seeing, are, mirrors, nature,* and *reflected* have poetic equivalents that the lexicographers do not put in their books. *Seeing* is *imagining* and some form of this word governs the definition of all these terms, but none of them predicates a disregard for the facts of reality. The poetical thinker sees the facts of reality as they are; that is, he sees them out of context. The logical thinkers—historians, philosophers, and scientists—are far less realistic than poets in that they invariably attempt to supply a context which at heart they know does not exist.

One of the gravest tasks of the poet is, consequently, to write a continuous nervous commentary on the thinking of all the non-poets. He must always labor to preserve the fragments of reality in their familiar form in order to keep them from being dissolved into the nothingness, which is a way of saying the rigid systematization, of logical sequences. In other words, the poet once again sees a world in which, like that of the child, casual connections, formal relationships, whys and wherefores are unknown and unwanted. His eyes are unprejudiced by the categories of analysis. His other senses share in the triumph of his eyes, and his imagination creates a new world. Since each poet lives for a moment in this special world and since each poem is a detached and separate thing shown to us by the poet, poetry has never progressed in the sense that history, philosophy, and science have. We can say Ptolemy, Copernicus, Galileo, Kepler, Newton and each name improves its predecessor; but when we say Homer, Dante, Shakespeare, Milton, Goethe, there is only consonance. Poetry really never grows up, for its very existence depends on a constant renewal of its youth.

By regularly renewing its youth, poetry is able to see each day as if it were the first morning of creation. Because of this constant sense of a newly created world, the poet, too, helps in the creation. Sidney, from whom I chose my text on poetry as a form of faith, makes this point as well, saying that thanks to the divine breath in him, the poet is able to bring forth things "far surpassing" the works of nature. When he writes this, he is modestly rephrasing the words of the poet-critic Scaliger.

> The poet makes another nature and other outcomes for men's acts, and finally, in the same way, makes himself another God. The other sciences are users of what the maker of them produced; but poetry, when it so splendidly gives the appearance of the things that are and of those that are not, seems not to narrate the events as the historians do, but to produce them as a God.

This statement may strike us as lacking in reverence, but in our fathers' thesaurus of metaphors God was often given the name of poet, and the poet and artist was often compared to God. The authority for the comparison began with a text in Plotinus, but Western man fully believed that the Greek Church confessed that it "believed in God the Father, Poet of Heaven and Earth." The obvious error in translation was not, I think, the result of an inadequate knowledge of Greek. There was a firm desire to mistranslate because men wanted God to be a poet and his creation to be a poem. "Then in forming man," says the Italian, Guarini, "the divine voice of the same divine poet indicated that he was pleased with the work of imitation, saying: 'Let us make man in our own image.'"

The connection between God and his mortal analogy, the poet, is described by Shakespeare in a passage so familiar that few readers have bothered to understand it.

> The poet's eye in a fine frenzy rolling,
> Doth glance from heaven to earth, from earth to heaven
> And as imagination bodies forth
> The forms of things unknown, the poet's pen
> Turns them to shapes and gives to airy nothing
> A local habitation and a name.

Because Duke Theseus of *A Midsummer-Night's Dream* speaks in an apparently derogatory fashion, this speech has long been regarded as a jest at the expense of poets. But we must remember that the whole temper of the play belies everything that critics make the Duke say and that Shakespeare carefully distinguishes between the imagination of the poet, the lunatic, and the lover by assigning to the poet a " fine frenzy " just as Drayton, in praising Marlowe, alludes to his " fine madness." But Shakespeare, I expect, goes beyond this to establish a divine analogy.

The world, said the Renaissance, is a poem that may be read in any order—up and down, down and up, forward and backward, backward and forward. Tasso elaborates on this by describing creation as an infinitely ordered epic, with all its parts bound together by a joyous concordance; " while there is nothing lacking in it, yet there is nothing there that does not serve for necessity of ornament." God, who is capable of unending variety and whose similes are things, ornaments the great poem he has written from top to bottom. This poem of creation Shakespeare says, may be read in all directions by the " rolling eye " of the lesser poet. But the poet, unlike God, has only similes with which to express things, but in compensation, like God, he can bring from " airy nothing " the " forms of things unknown." This is for Shakespeare the necessary equation. The poet is God's metaphor; he can create a new world from the great void.

But the world that the poet creates is not the world in which the laws of the scientist, the historian, or the philosopher flourish. It is not a world of firm assertion, but a world of interrogatory thought, for the poet is always the true questioner of the nature of the world that he makes. In general, he is content to stand before it and ask himself what it is, for his whole art depends on the questions that he frames in the tense moment of poetical thought. He understands, too, that it is the correctness of the questions that really matters. In the world that he creates by preserving its separateness, questions and answers are the same. He knows, too, that the propriety of his questions depends to a large degree on his consciousness of the facts of his non-poetic life. So the poet, like the child, is forever interrogating his universe and forever rejecting the answers that logical thinkers are only too eager to give him. Sensing reality for what it is, he has always known that the answers that man invents are imposed on reality and not contained in it. Truth stands in this and in this alone. So the poet understands that the chase is a false hunt and that man at his best can only construct fitting inquiries about the isolated experiences that he has chosen to call reality. This is the end of poetical thinking and the wisdom that is poetry.

But what I have been saying about the nature of poetical thought has probably no validity at all because I write entirely without poetical experience. I have put myself by my own words in the room of those who attempt some kind of logic and who are excluded thereby from the chambers inhabited by poets. Fortunately, I can be corrected, and the four poets, whose remarks on poets and poetry I have attempted to introduce, will shortly see to that.

R. P. Blackmur

Edwin Muir:

between the

Tiger's Paws

YOUNG ENGLISHMEN, WHEN asked how they felt about the poetry of Edwin Muir, answered by and large that they had not troubled to make an opinion about it because it had little relation to the serious venture of poetry at this time. There was an intonation of voice that if prompted to make an opinion, it would be a bad one. Young Americans, when asked, returned a restive blankness, rather like the puppy who does not understand what is wanted, and the Americans, in this case, were nearer right than the English if only because they had nothing at all to go on, and the Englishmen (so we like to think) ought to have known better as a race of people given to the making of verse: of making something into verse; a habit which has occasionally produced poetry. I would say that the Americans needed instruction, while the English needed correction about matters of fact. There is something wrong about habits of writing and reading poetry which insist on valuing highly only the professional poetry which springs (when it does not merely make a bog) from those habits.

The professional poet and his poetry should be seen as the collapsing chimaeras they mainly, and of necessity, are; then we could scratch where we itch. Then, too, we could enjoy for the hard and interesting things *they* are the verses made by quite unprofessional poets like Edwin Muir out of honest and endless effort and the general materials of their language. In this case, most of us who write would even appreciate ourselves better and would do better what we did and would above all appreciate better the true great poet and how he differs from us only, and enormously, in degree. "*Onorate l'altissimo poeta; l'ombra sua torna, ch'era dipartita.*" Your small poet shares in that honor.

It is only degree. Think of Edwin Muir and listen to these words. "Through all [these images] there runs a feeling, a feeling which is our own no less than the poet's, a human feeling of bitter memories, of shuddering horror, of melancholy, of homesickness, of tenderness, of a kind of childish *pietás* that could prompt this vain revival of things perished, these playthings fashioned by a religious devotion . . . ." No words could better be applied to the praise of Edwin Muir than these; I would alter nothing and add very little, as the remainder of these remarks, of which they will form the burden, will show. But the words were not written about Muir but about a passage in the *Aeneid* to exemplify the complex of images and the spirit which animates them which inhabit all poetry, and they were written [in the *Encyclopedia Britannica*, article "Aesthetics"] by Benedetto Croce. They touch on the point of projection where Muir and Virgil join in kind however distant they may be in degree.

Virgil wrote the will of the Roman Empire when that empire was young. Muir, sturdy in his own way, has written an individual, a personal—an English, a Scotch—footnote to life in the

true empire at a time when the notion of a good empire seems
no longer plausible or possible but only an image for longing
without hope. There is nothing either official or evangelical or
prophetic about him, and least of all is there any plea for the
kind of greatness we call grandeur, public or private. There is,
rather, all Virgil's piety—the childish *pietás*, as Croce puts it—
directed inwards upon the force of his own mind and thence
outwards upon the nature—the naturalist's nature and human
nature—that has affected him. Piety is that medium of conduct
in which we feel and then achieve a harmony in the clashing of
necessities: that harmony which I find myself calling over and
over the concert of conflicts, and which is so difficult to achieve
without the mediating presence of some form of empire, Roman
or not. This difficulty in achieving harmony indeed seems the
characteristic difficulty of the human condition in our times, and
it sometimes seems possible only to think it in verse.

To say that this is what Muir has done is another way of
saying something about the attractive force of Muir's verse: he
has made his harmony in the thought—not the numbers, the
thought—of his verse. Verse for him is the mode of his thought-
ful piety, the mode of the mind's action, where his piety is not
only enacted for him but takes independent action on its own
account and for us: when it does, it becomes poetry. This differs
from the usual run of things. Usually, poetry gets along very
well only reflecting thought already entertained or so to speak
without any primary thought at all. I do not say that Muir's
mode is any better, only that it is worth distinguishing how it is
different from, say, the poetry of Ezra Pound or that of Pope.
Pound's thought is in his cadence and numbers; Pope's versifi-
cation cuts off the roots of his thought; Muir's thought is in the
verse itself—hence the sense in the most regular of his verses of

a continuous vital irregularity, whereby we know how alien and independent is thought that has taken on its identity, and how full of war any harmony is in its incarnations.

There is a passage in the chapter on Rome in Muir's auto-biography which bears on the point. It is not, of course, verse, and rings in the " other harmony " of prose. But it leads of a certainty towards poetry, purely and without infection; which is one reason I quote it, with the second reason that my own sense of Rome is in good part Muir's and that in his language he has discovered for me a grand version of the experience I stood con-victed of in Rome. I refer to the current of thought which he communicates in the word *Incarnation*. Rome is where all man-ner of things take to the grace of the body, body in their meet-ings and body in their conflicts, a concert altogether.

We saw the usual sights [he says], sometimes enchanted, sometimes disappointed; but it was Rome itself that took us, the riches stored in it, the ages assembled in a tumultuous order, the vistas at street corners where one looked across from one century to another, the innumerable churches, palaces, squares, fountains, monuments, ruins; and the Romans themselves going about their business as if this were the natural and right setting for the life of mankind.

The history of Rome is drenched in blood and blackened with crime; yet all that seemed to be left now was the peace of memory. As we wandered about the Forum we could not summon up the blood-stained ghosts; they had quite gone, bleached by centuries into a luminous transparency, or evapo-rated into the bright still air. Their works were there, but these cast only the ordinary shadow which everything set up by mankind gathers at its foot. The grass in the courtyard of the Temple of the Vestals seemed to be drenched in peace down to the very root, and it was easy to imagine gods and men still in friendly talk together there.

So far the harmony is easy and no more than sensitive to contrive. "But," he goes on, "it was the evidence of another Incarnation that met one everywhere and gradually exerted its influence." Here Muir reminds himself of the life neighboring the Scotch churches of his boyhood in the persons of their ministers. "In figures such as these the Word became something more than a word in my childish mind; but nothing told me that Christ was born in the flesh and lived on the earth.

In Rome that image was to be seen everywhere, not only in churches, but on the walls of houses, at cross-roads in the suburbs, in wayside shrines in the parks, and in private rooms. I remember stopping for a long time one day to look at a little plaque on the wall of a house in the Via degli Artisti, representing the Annunciation. An angel and a young girl, their bodies inclined toward each other, their knees bent as if they were overcome by love, 'tutto tremante,' gazed upon each other like Dante's pair; and that representation of a human love so intense that it could not reach farther seemed the perfect earthly symbol of the love that passes understanding. . . . That these images should appear everywhere, reminding everyone of the Incarnation, seemed to me natural and right, just as it was right that my Italian friends should step out frankly into life. This open declaration was to me the very mark of Christianity, distinguishing it from the older religions.

The harmony is harder here since it has to do with how harmonies are come by, with the art of the art, the passion of the passion, the story of the story. It is like—as a direct experience—St. Thomas' definition of allegory where the words signify things which themselves then signify further, yet there remain with us only the primitive words or the plaque on the wall. The allegory which Rome provided for Muir out of the monuments and fountains of human ruins and aspirations, and which he records in his prose, is a kind of prefiguration of the allegory—the effort to make things speak further for themselves than our mere words can signify alone—which he completes in his verse. I should like to point out that these allegories are not—as so many of our allegories are nowadays—puzzles or evasions or deliberate ambiguities or veilings of purpose, and they do not require interpretation according to anything but the sense of intimacy in experience approached or observed with piety in order to accept what is there. All that is needed are the common terms of our tradition together with some familiarity with the habits of English verse and a responsiveness to a handful of literary allusions which are, or used to be, universally permitted and expected. I mean the allusions which are very nearly a part of the substance of our mind, so early were they bred in us by education and conversation: the allusions we can make without consciousness of their meanings, but which, when we do become conscious of their meanings, are like thunder and lightning and the letting go of breath. A thing is what it is, and is its own meaning, which might seem to us, as it did to Dante in his *Paradiso*, a condition of blessedness, though in our context of reading and writing we take tautology as the face of obfuscation and irrelevance. Ripeness is all. A thing is what it is, and when you can say so you will have made an allegory of direct statement—a statement so full of itself that it promises an ultimate comprehensibility; it prefigures what is in its nature to be fulfilled, either backwards or forwards, as is just.

Here is such an example of direct allegory, the last quatrain of "The Good Man in Hell":

> One doubt of evil would bring down such a grace,
>   Open such a gate, all Eden could enter in,
> Hell be a place like any other place,
>   And love and hate and life and death begin.

This looks backwards, through a little theology, into our most backward selves where we abort, but need not, human action in the hell of the willfully wrong affirmation: it is that lethargy of sensation, or boredom of perception, which feels only the wrong good. Here is another allegory, which though it returns to Homer, had better be said to look forward. The poem is called "The Return," and it may be that the final phase of our pilgrimage, whatever earlier routes it took, is always a return, at least it would seem so to those of us in middle age or beyond. To the Ulysses who wanes in each of us in long hankering there is Penelope waxing ahead: the *gnostos*, the home-coming, the return, which constitutes by magic certainty, like the octave in music, the farthest reach of the journey.

> The doors flapped open in Ulysses' house,
> The lolling latches gave to every hand,
> Let traitor, babbler, tout and bargainer in.
> The rooms and passages resounded
> With ease and chaos of a public market,
> The walls mere walls to lean on as you talked,
> Spat on the floor, surveyed some newcomer
> With an absent eye. There you could be yourself.
> Dust in the nooks, weeds nodding in the yard,
> The thick walls crumbling. Even the cattle came
> About the doors with mild familiar stare
> As if this were their place.
> All around the island stretched the clean blue sea.
>
> Sole at the house's heart Penelope
> Sat at her chosen task, endless undoing
> Of endless doing, endless weaving, unweaving,
> In the clean chamber. Still her loom ran empty
> Day after day. She thought: "Here I do nothing
> Or less than nothing, making an emptiness
> Amid disorder, weaving, unweaving the lie

The day demands. Ulysses, this is duty,
To do and undo, to keep a vacant gate
Where order and right and hope and peace can enter.
Oh will you ever return? Or are you dead,
And this wrought emptiness my ultimate emptiness? "

She wove and unwove and wove and did not know
That even then Ulysses on the long
And winding road of the world was on his way.

This poem needs no commentary by way of discussion, for it invites the comment of attachment, of intimacy. It is a plaque of incarnation affixed to the wall of the mind, where, looking, you could be yourself. There is no end to the journey that is at hand. Let us say that this is a poem of great tenderness, the tenderness of human action which stretches between one being and another and stretches most in absence, most of all in the absence in the same room, and yet is the tenderness, which is the life, of actual possibility, confirming it even in the snapping point of failure. In our beginnings are our ends, all a return. To repeat, if the good man in hell broke lethargy, Penelope creates the live waiting which is also attention commanded. Each is annunciation bringing incarnation.

If so the poems themselves are epiphanies, like those green ones Stephen Dedalus meant to write, for epiphany—the showing of what is already made—is as far as the mind can go with what is wanted or needed. The verse makes only the analogous incarnation of the thing—its mere behavior—into words and forms that sometimes become poetry. But the secondary often leads us back to the primary, to what is still first; so let us look a little at the kind of poet Muir is, at his equipment in verse, and at the ideas and habits of mind that beset him in his epiphany of his grand theme.

As to the kind of poetry which Muir writes, it is the kind we all live in our salutations, our aversions, and our reveries—when we cry out, turn aside, or let the dreams within us work themselves into shape beyond our normal shaping powers. He is like all of us in those moments when we put meaning into our words. Only he is better than most of us are, for the shapes and meanings last for others' use: they become common currency in motion. There are no monuments here, either of imagination or ambition, and no bids for power and domination. There are, rather, gestures of recognition and intimations of the forms of all these. We are in their presence, as Shakespeare says water is in water, or as Burns says the snowflakes are on the black river. Only it is not Shakespeare and not Burns. This is what is meant by saying that Muir is not a professional poet, not even a public poet. Neither the open nor the overweening career was ever his. This is not Milton, who knew and overpassed his powers, but Milton's secretary, the Member from Hull, Andrew Marvell, who pursued his best possibilities and was several times seized by powers beyond himself—the same powers that sometimes seize us. Or let us say that Muir is like Traherne, who rehearsed traditional mysteries, rather than like Donne, for whom none of the traditions and no mere rehearsal was ever enough. Perhaps Muir is like George Herbert without a parish or a doctrine or any one temple to construct. He made secular what was his own, which was indeed how he saw it even when it was supernatural in its mode of contact, in annunciation and resurrection. His poems and no doubt his life were topical only to himself, and we make him our topic in the common place between us. He made a commonplace book in our own language.

Such is Muir's kind of poetry, and there ought to be a name for the kind. No doubt Mr. Northrop Frye will provide us with a good one (for he knows how we take hold of things better by a name than by the substance), but in the meantime we can say that it springs from an old and natural tradition like sunlight or breathing and is about as hard to do without, until we take our summers on the moon. I think there would be neither great poetry nor amusing poetry nor the grand folly of private poetry if there were not also—aware of all these—the steady poetry of the kind written by Muir. This poetry is a kind of thinking in verse, which is a very different thing from versifying thought, for the verse is the vital mode rather than the mere mode of the thought and is thus the substance of what we remember as well as the memorable form. It is a thinking in verse—as thinking in algebra or in farming or in love—which so far as it reaches form is poetry alive with the action of the mind, and which when it does not reach form has the dullness of the active mind failing. Almost none of our brains, as Darwin knew, are good for very much thinking, in verse or otherwise. Thoughts that fail in poetry are like dogs that have lost the scent.

Some brook has run between or a swamp sogs under the feet, and the life runs out of the flurry of action. Where the hound gives up and denies his interest the poet goes on willy-nilly, more dogged than any dog, so long as there is any verse to help him pretend a course or a spoor. Somewhere, across some gap or dark occasion, what is lost may be recovered. I take it Muir means something like this in another language—which has the desperateness of the certainty of what approaches saying and cannot be said—when he ends his autobiography in the following way:

> In the infinite web of things and events chance must be something different from what we think it to be. To comprehend that is not given to us, and to think of it is to recognize a

mystery, and to acknowledge the necessity of faith. As I look back on the part of the mystery which is my own life, my own fable, what I am most aware of is that we receive more than we can ever give; we receive it from the past, on which we draw with every breath, but also—and this is a point of faith—from the Source of the mystery itself, by the means which religious people call Grace.

Muir was looking back at the perennial mystery, and perhaps the perennial philosophy, of his whole life; I am looking at the mystery of the practice of writing verse. There is some place where the views cross.

One such place perhaps may be seen in the type of verse which Muir characteristically writes when the verse comes nearest to thought—when the words contribute to and indeed almost occasion the thought. The words precipitate, they do not distill the thought. Muir makes no epigrams in the modern sense in words which in themselves flash the wit; as a poet he is singularly little in love with words, and his words never make us blush. He makes no apothegms nor gnostic sayings either; there is no special penetration and no special mystery of knowledge; he observes by habit, rather, that way of words which goes with ritual and makes runes: he makes an old script, an older and different alphabet, out of the general mystery and the common institution, inescapably present, when looked at, in our regular vocabulary of word and myth and attitude. He has the great advantage of the power to re-create or transform them. His own poems make the best commentary on the distinction I want to set forth. Here is the end of " Ballad of Hector in Hades ":

> Two shadows racing on the grass,
>   Silent and so near,
> Until his shadow falls on mine.
>   And I am rid of fear.

> The race is ended. Far away
>   I hang and do not care,
> While round bright Troy Achilles whirls
>   A corpse with streaming hair.

One does not even need to have read the *Iliad*, unless as a child; everything to do with Troy is part of our natural possession—a gift of our past—and all our languages have so constantly, if irregularly, repossessed themselves of it that every fresh statement of it, every variation or addition, has a natural authenticity. Hector and Achilles might well have been taken up by Freud along with Oedipus and Narcissus, for at least within our psyches we all run in great heat around that wall, and it makes little difference whether the other fellow is Hector or Achilles. In the eschatology of the psyche, Hades is not so judgmatical as the Christian hell, and our roles continue to reverse themselves, nightmare to nightmare, as they do in ordinary life. Our nightmares are the playmasters of our minds, and none are so masterly as our Greek nightmares. Homer has them all in their urgent and obliterative forms; Ovid their urbane forms; Muir, when he tackles them in his verse, their therapeutic and reminding forms.

Surely there is no cliché of nightmare so universal, touching so sharply upon us all, as the corpse with streaming hair; Achilles (and it could have been Hector) in this poem is only a *figura* for the figures with whom we are in perpetual pursuit in our private Hades. It is our nightmares which wake us as we have lost our next-to-last breath, and with what is left we make a rune or die, and there is a wide emptiness all around us, in which our senses and our decisions swim in common vertigo, accusing and self-accusing. This is the rune for the corpse with the streaming hair; and I will only remind you that the Duke of Clarence, just before he was visited by his murderers, saw in that dream of

his which " lengthened after life " (*Richard the Third*, I, iv)
" A shadow like an angel, with bright hair / Dabbled in blood."
Clarence, like Hector, spoke from the private Hades of the
psyche, and he, too, made a rune.

From " The Enchanted Knight " I quote the first and the last
two stanzas.

> Lulled by La Belle Dame Sans Merci he lies
>   In the bare wood below the blackening hill.
> The plough drives nearer now, the shadow flies.
>   Past him across the plain, but he lies still.
>
>   .   .   .   .   .
>
> When a bird cries within the silent grove
>   The long-lost voice goes by, he makes to rise
> And follow, but his cold limbs never move,
>   And on the turf unstirred his shadow lies.
>
> But if a withered leaf should drift
>   Across his face and rest, the dread drops start
> Chill on his forehead. Now he tries to lift
>   The insulting weight that stays and breaks his heart.

No one needs to know Keats's poem, any more than Keats
needed to know the literary and folk sources for the belief in
the fatal destructiveness of love in one of its roles upon which his
poem—and Muir's—depends. The belief had a cave home in
some furthest source within us—perhaps in some anterior metamorphosis of the psyche in which love and its inspirations
exacted their cost more vividly than now and charged daring
more quickly with its natural end. As we think in an earlier
form of ourselves, so we use a different alphabet of feelings; and
in that form and that alphabet we believe preciously in what
in its present form we greet only with the attraction of horror.
The verse restores the early form by giving its thought a mode

of action. All Muir's poem except one word is a rune and ritual celebration of that dread lady—Robert Graves's White Goddess—who takes back in one moment not only her gift to her lover but also his life itself; the one word is the word "insulting," a modern and moody word, by which the poet expresses his rebellion against the tradition and his denial of the ritual, the while it breaks him down. It is as if Muir thought for a moment like Dostoevsky, where the last gasp of the individual is in insult and injury and laceration. The history of the word "insult" is present here whether Muir knew it or not: as a frequentative form of the verb *insilare*, to leap upon. The rain of insult is perpetual while life lasts. This poem, then, is a rune in old ballad form, to express and purge the nightmare of the White Goddess.

The poem called "The Island" goes beyond the condition of rune and makes a spell out of the glamour or secret art of grammar. The island of the title is not Muir's birthplace, the island of Orkney, but Sicily, the visible merging place for all our histories, teeming as it does with living people, with the races and beliefs and arts of other times, especially teeming with beliefs, some now quite lost to conscious memory. In Sicily erosion and fertility compete in every mode: "Harvests of men to give men birth." All this is only less so for the island of Orkney, for we survive, as it were, only in islands. Here is the end of the poem.

> And self-begotten cycles close
> About our way; indigenous art
> And simple spells make unafraid
> The haunted labyrinths of the heart,
> And with our wild succession braid
> The resurrection of the rose.

Possibly it should be emphasized that it is the indigenous art and the simple spells that make the braid. Indigenous art is innate form. To make the indigenous simple is to make the spell of rational imagination with which both to purge and to involve our wild succession.

That is to say, in the work of a man like Muir whose mind has no temptation either to remake the world or to reason it out of existence, the rational imagination here makes its maximum task to recapture tradition in direct apprehension, to find in what happens to him an Illumination in the linkage of the chances that have gone before with the abstractions that persist. It is as if, with Muir, allegory were the indigenous and final art. As he says,

> Or so I dream when at my door
> I hear my soul, my visitor.

And when he says this he reminds us of Emily Dickinson and how we might reassess her along the same lines, but with a different and perhaps larger stretch, as those that contain Muir. Muir is a Dickinson with a different deficiency. But both poets resorted naturally to all the tradition to which they were exposed, and they made their resort to find abstractions in which their problematic—even their unseemly—sensibilities could be united with their selves. Muir's resort was to the Greek and classical, to the Christian, and to the monstrous forms or postures of the psyche that precede all our taxonomy, and it is these forms that he set about putting to the commonest musics he could find: the sonnet, the ballad, the anecdote, and the commonest diction he could hear—not the language of the street, but the general language of literature. The two provided means for the discernment of the memorable, since it was in the service of memory that both had grown up. Here one thinks of Valéry's remark, that one keeps in memory only what one has not understood, or of that poet's other remark that Reason (and this is her warrant of office) admires the monuments (the cities of imagination) that she could not herself have built. In Muir it is sometimes the actual damaged monuments of true cities only in our lifetime truncated from their stories, like the city of Prague, which he loved, and which is the subject of the poem, "The Good Town." Plato, Augustine, Dante and (in a small, persistent pang) Baudelaire did this, and so Muir. Cities are like annunciations, visits of the soul on our grandest human scale in monumental analogy to the everlasting devastations of the moment seized.

> Whether the soul at first
> This pilgrimage began,
> Or the shy body leading
> Conducted soul to soul
> Who knows? This is the most
> That soul and body can,
> To make us each for each
> And in our spirit whole.

These lines, which end a poem called "The Annunciation," make a wooing of that goddess, other than the White Goddess who makes us die, who makes us live, the personal city within the great. There is a poem called simply "Song"—the simple spell of indigenous art—where the two cities are in piety joined. It is the song of the thought Muir put most in his verse.

> The quarrel from the start,
> Long past and never past,
> The war of mind and heart,
> The great war and the small
> That tumbles the hovel down
> And topples town on town
> Come to one place at last:
> Love gathers all.

One observes here that Muir's most direct statement reaches to
the purest abstraction. He is like this even when his concern
is in the immediate mood of the crash of melancholy and joy.
I would cite, for they are too much to repeat here in full, the
ends of the twin poems called " Dejection " and " Sorrow."

> For every eloquent voice dies in this air
> Wafted from anywhere to anywhere
> And never counted by the careful clock,
> That cannot strike the hour
> Of power that will dissolve this power
> Until the rock rise up and split the rock.

> ———

> If it were only so . . .
> But right and left I find
> Sorrow, sorrow,
> And cannot be resigned,
> Knowing that we were made
> By joy to drive joy's trade
> And not to waver to and fro,
> But quickly go.

It was just said that these things are in piety joined, and piety
is not an artichoke to be pulled apart for the eating, with the
most part discarded. We have here, in the language of Croce
about Virgil, which we began by quoting, " a human feeling of
bitter memories, of shuddering horror, of melancholy, of homesickness, of tenderness, of a kind of childish pietás "; and we
must not tamper with it like psychiatrists, but become intimate
with it without assault, like fellow-humans. It is with piety
that we recognize our familiars, even when they are horrors or
our inmost selves, but most when we see we should be nothing
at all without them. It is with piety that we make the best order
out of our stories. If we need an abstraction or a generalization

to grasp and share what Muir's thinking in verse is up to, it is in our best conception of the piety of the story. For there is a piety in Muir—and like humility, in a hair's breadth it will be pride or humiliation—towards nature, the cross, the Greeks, death, time, love, old age, and to the obsessions of all these and their nightmares. For our nightmares only smother us where we have paid too much attention to our real life.

Now to repeat, since even a story must repeat itself to be true, wherever Mr. Muir himself is, the inner motion of his poetry still draws from the "carnival of birth and death," as he calls it, of the Orkney sea-farm where he grew up. Muir is an island man and is full of natural piety—a phrase Wordsworth put into poetry. But where Wordsworth observed it, and sought it, Muir's poems exert his natural piety, as a function of his being; exert it equally to the hill and the plough, to the stars and to his Visitor, the Soul, never forgetting the one when he greets the other. His poetry participates without prejudice in the warfare between the two elements of the tradition which moves him. I do not think this warfare very different from the war of the journey and the war of the pity which inhabited the mind of Dante, and I think it is in this sense that Muir is a traditional poet; he deals with the wars of our journey and our pity. His order—whether in his prosody of ballad and sonnet and blank verse or in his themes of the human condition—is as old as the terms of experience and the reach of thought; but everywhere there is the wildness of fresh disorder which is the current of life in his order. If the wildness is reminiscent of eternity both before and after, so much the better. The regular is most wild.

All this is vivid in the poems themselves. Here is the other of the two poems he has called "The Return." (The first was that with which we began, regarding Penelope awaiting Ulysses.)

> . . . And the voices,
> Sweeter than any sound dreamt of or known,
> Call me, recall me. I draw near at last,
> An old old man, and scan the ancient walls
> Rounded and softened by the compassionate years,
> The old and heavy and long-leaved trees that watch
> This my inheritance in friendly darkness.
> And yet I cannot enter, for all within
> Rises before me there, rises against me,
> A sweet and terrible labyrinth of longing,
> So that I turn aside and take the road
> That always, early or late, runs on before.

And here are the last distichs of "Epitaph" and "Comfort in Self-Despite."

> If now is Resurrection, then let stay
> Only what's ours when this is put away.

> ———

> So I may yet recover by this bad
> Research that good I scarcely dreamt I had.

In Mr. J. C. Hall's introduction to the *Collected Poems*, Stephen Spender is quoted as saying that Muir witnessed everywhere in Rome the climactic symbol of Resurrection. To this Mr. Hall adds a footnote. "Edwin Muir tells me that the symbol which impressed him in Rome was that of Incarnation, not Resurrection." To me, both seem right, and the two fragments of verse which I have just read attest it. In Muir's poems both Resurrection and Incarnation—the rediscovery and the bodying forth—are going on at the same time. That is why so much of the poetry is nearly not words at all, but the action of the mind itself taking thought of Resurrection and Incarnation, the carnival of birth and death. Like Prospero, that great persona of human piety, this poet would still his beating mind.

> This love a moment known
> For what I do not know
> And in a moment gone
> Is like the happy doe
> That keeps its perfect laws
> Between the tiger's paws
> And vindicates its cause.

Between the tiger's paws Muir stills his beating mind.

Yvor Winters

Poetic
Styles,
Old and New

THE SHORT POEM OF THE LATE
middle ages, of the sixteenth
century, and of the early seven-
teenth century was usually rational in structure, and in fact was
very often logical. This structure began to break down toward
the middle of the seventeenth century: the signs are most obvious in *Lycidas*, but one can find them in Marvell and Vaughan
and elsewhere. The rational structure was often used for un-
reasonable ends, as in much of Sidney and Donne, but the
structure is almost always there. These facts are well known
to scholars by now, and they may seem unworthy of mention;
but they appear to be unknown to many of our critics, and I
need to call attention to them for the sake of what I shall say
later. Within this rational frame, however, there were two main
schools of poetry in the sixteenth century and earlier: on the
one hand there were the poets of the plain style, and on the
other hand the poets of the style which has been variously
labeled courtly, ornate, sugared, or Petrarchan. Some poets employed both methods, but most poets worked mainly in one or

the other, for the difference was a difference of principle, and the principles were commonly understood. Wyatt, Gascoigne, Raleigh, Greville, and Jonson wrote mainly in the plain style. Sidney and Spenser can serve as examples of the courtly.

Donne can hardly be described as courtly or sugared, but he is ornate, and to this extent Petrarchan. Donne is only superficially a rebel against the tradition of Sidney; essentially he is a continuator, at least in a large number of his poems. His mind is more complex than that of Sidney, and more profound; his temperament is more violent and more perverse; his virtues and his vices are more striking; but in most of his famous poems he is working in the same tradition. At this time I can refer to only one of his poems: the *Valediction Forbidding Mourning*.

The poem is so well known that I need not quote it. The entire poem, like most of Donne's poems, is hyperbolic: he overstates his case violently, in a manner which, in our time, is called dramatic. The theme of the poem, though fairly serious, is also simple: that is, the lovers are united by their rational souls rather than by their sensible souls, and their love is therefore relatively stable, and they can endure a physical parting more easily than can those lovers who are united merely by sense. This idea in itself is an overstatement, and Donne, of all people, must have been aware of the fact: this overstatement is part of the hyperbole. But there is more than this in the hyperbole: there are the metaphors and similes. The figures in the first twelve lines are both trite and ridiculous. Mr. Cleanth Brooks says that some of the same figures in *The Canonization* are offered as parody; I doubt this, but they are not offered as parody here. They are offered here in absolute seriousness, and they are bad. But this is not the main point, as far as I am concerned at present. The main point is that they are ornament, decoration.

They say very little about the subject, say it loosely, and say it with a kind of naïve violence. Jonson could have said more in two lines than Donne says in twelve.

The decoration in the opening lines is bad decoration, but later the decoration is good. The gold and the compasses are brilliant and they have made the poem famous; nevertheless, the gold and the compasses are decoration. The gold and the compasses tell us nothing about the lovers, really, except that they are inseparable in terms of the rational soul, yet the gold and the compasses are sensory details. There is much reference to sensory—usually visual—detail in Renaissance poetry which is not meant to be visualized; I shall have more to say of this later. But the gold and the compasses are meant to be visualized, or if they are not so meant, Donne out-did himself. Yet we do not visualize the lovers either as gold or as compasses: if we did so, the poem would become preposterous. We visualize the gold and the compasses and between these and the lovers there is a very general, an almost uncertain, intellectual correspondence. It is the gold and the compasses which save these passages, and very nearly in their own right. The passages are ornament, or very nearly so. They are very quotable, and have often been quoted. They are quotable because they are detachable; they are detachable because they are attached.

It is foolish to say, with Mr. Eliot, that Donne thinks with his sense (that is, his sensible soul); he thinks with his rational soul, and he often ornaments his thought with his sensory perception, sometimes well and sometimes badly. The formula is Horatian: profit and pleasure—profit from reason, pleasure from sensory perception or other decoration. The formula is common in the Renaissance, but it is not the only formula possible in the Renaissance or at other times. The formula of our own time which corresponds in part to the Horatian formula is that of tenor and vehicle, although the modern formula has a wider applicability. In Donne's poem the constancy of the lovers is the tenor; the gold and the compasses are vehicles; the vehicles are more interesting than the tenor; therefore they are ornament, and the tenor—the essential theme—suffers. In our time the most famous Renaissance vehicle, as far as I know, has been Marvell's chariot. It functions in much the same way as Donne's gold and compasses.

In Shakespeare's sonnets we find both plain and ornate styles, sometimes in the same poem, but both, more often than not, in a state of decay; and we find also the only decay of rational structure which I can recollect among the major poets of the time. I intend now to discuss some of Shakespeare's sonnets, and next two of Jonson's major poems, and then to draw a few conclusions.

II

There are few of Shakespeare's sonnets which do not show traces of genius, and genius of an unusually beguiling kind; and in a fair number we have more than traces. Yet in the past ten years or so I have found them more and more disappointing.[1]

In the first place there is in a large number of the poems an attitude of servile weakness on the part of the poet in the face of the person addressed; this attitude is commonly so marked

[1] John Crowe Ransom antedates me by quite a few years in this heresy. See his essay "Shakespeare at Sonnets" in *The World's Body* (1938). Ransom's objections and my own are similar in some respects and different in others. My own tardiness in seeing Shakespeare's weaknesses is evidence (a) of the effect of established habit on critical judgment and (b) of the curious way in which a shifting mixture of the good and the bad can produce a result which it is difficult to judge objectively.

as to render a sympathetic approach to the subject all but impossible, in spite of any fragmentary brilliance which may be exhibited. It will not do to reply that this is a convention of the courtly style and should not be taken seriously. If it is a convention of the courtly style, then it is a weakness in that style. But it is not an invariable quality of the courtly poets; it occurs very seldom in poets of the plain style; and Shakespeare seems to mean it seriously.

In the second place, Shakespeare seldom takes the sonnet form with any real seriousness. The sonnets are almost invariably conceived in very simple terms and are developed through simple repetition or antithesis, so that they never achieve the closely organized treatment of the subject which we find in the best of Jonson and Donne. This weakness is often aggravated by the fact that Shakespeare frequently poses his problem and then solves it by an evasion or an irrelevant cliché: this is more or less the method of the courtly style at its weakest, but the element of genius which goes into many of these sonnets raises one's expectations to the point that one cannot take this sort of triviality with good grace.

In the third place, Shakespeare often allows his sensitivity to the connotative power of language to blind him to the necessity for sharp denotation, with the result that a line or passage or even a whole poem may disappear behind a veil of uncertainty: in this last weakness he is even farther from his major contemporaries than in any of the others. I shall endeavor to illustrate these weaknesses as they occur in poems which I shall discuss.

I will begin with LXVI:

> Tir'd with all these, for restful death I cry
> As to behold desert a beggar born,

And needy nothing trimm'd in jollity,
And purest faith unhappily forsworn,
And gilded honor shamefully misplac'd,
And maiden virtue rudely strumpeted,
And right perfection wrongfully disgrac'd,
And strength by limping sway disabled,
And art made tongue-tied by authority,
And folly—doctor-like—controlling skill,
And simple truth miscalled simplicity,
And captive good attending captain ill:
    Tir'd with all these, from these I would be gone,
    Save that, to die, I leave my love alone.

This is one of a number of Elizabethan poems dealing with dis-illusionment with the world. Others are Gascoigne's "Wood-manship," "The Lie" by Raleigh, and "False world, goodnight," by Ben Jonson. But whereas Gascoigne, Raleigh, and Jonson offer the best solutions that they can, Raleigh with righteous defiance, Gascoigne and Jonson with a combination of scorn for corruption and Christian acceptance of the individual fate, Shakespeare (like Arnold after him, in "Dover Beach") turns aside from the issues he has raised to a kind of despairing senti-mentality, and the effect is one of weakness, poetic and per-sonal. The same thing occurs in many other sonnets: for examples XXIX ("When in disgrace with fortune and men's eyes") and XXX ("When to the sessions of sweet silent thought"). I do not wish to deny the many felicities in these poems, for they are real; but the poems do not rise to the occa-sions which they invoke. The poem which I have just quoted would be a fine example of the plain style, except for the couplet, which represents sentimental degeneration of the courtly rhetoric.

It would be easy to make a list of inept phrases from the sonnets. The clichés, for example, are numerous and well known, and so are the bad plays on words ("When first your eye I eyed "). But most poets sin in this fashion much of the time, or in some comparable fashion. There is another kind of weak phrasing in Shakespeare, however, which is prevalent in his work and more serious than the cliché or the bad pun; it is characteristic of later ages rather than his own, and it sets him apart from his great contemporaries. This is his use of words for some vague connotative value, with little regard for exact denotation. An interesting example occurs in CXVI:

> Let me not to the marriage of true minds
> Admit impediments. Love is not love
> Which alters when it alteration finds,
> Or bends with the remover to remove:
> O no! it is an ever-fixed mark,
> That looks on tempests and is never shaken;
> It is the star to every wandering bark,
> Whose worth's unknown, although his height be taken.
> Love's not Time's fool, though rosy lips and cheeks
> Within his bending sickle's compass come;
> Love alters not with his brief hours and weeks,
> But bears it out even to the edge of doom.
>   If this be error and upon me proved,
>   I never writ, nor no man ever loved.

The difficulty here resides in the word *worth*. The fixed star, which guides the mariner, is compared to true love, which guides the lover. The mariner, by taking the height of the star, can estimate his position at sea, despite the fact that he knows nothing of the star's " worth." *Worth*, with reference to the star, probably means astrological influence, though it might mean something else. The lover, by fixing his mind on the concept of true love, similarly can guide himself in his personal life. But what does *worth*, as distinct from height, mean in this second connection? For the lover can scarcely guide himself by a concept of true love, he can scarcely indeed have a concept of true love, unless he has some idea of the worth of true love. The comparison blurs at this point, and with it the meaning. One may perhaps push the astrological influence here and say that the lover, although he has a general knowledge of the nature and virtue (if virtue can be separated from worth) of true love, yet does not know precisely the effect upon him that true love will have. But this will not do: he obviously knows something of the effect, for the rest of the poem says that he does. There is simply no such separation between the two functions of true love as there is between the two functions of the star, yet the comparison is made in such a way as to indicate a separation.

This kind of thing does not occur in Greville or Donne or Jonson. Even in the more ornate Sidney—for example in the clumsy figurative language of "Leave me, O love"—it is usually possible to follow the thought even though the figure may be mishandled. But here one loses the thought. Greville, in "Down in the depth," employs the language of theology; Donne employs the language of astrology (and other technical language) in the "Valediction of my Name in a Window." Nothing is lost by this precision, but on the contrary there is a gain, for the emotion cannot have force when its nature and origin are obscure. Shakespeare contents himself here with a vague feeling of the mysterious and the supernatural, and the feeling is very vague indeed.

The sonnet is characteristic in other respects. The successive quatrains do not really develop the theme; each restates it. This makes, perhaps, for easy absorption on the part of the more or less quiescent reader, but it makes also for a somewhat simple and uninteresting poetry. The sonnet form is short, and the

great poet should endeavor to use it more efficiently, to say as
much as can be said of his subject within its limits; such effi-
ciency is never characteristic of Shakespeare. Lines nine and ten
are clichés, which are barely rescued by an habitual grace, and
the concluding couplet is a mere tag, which has no dignity or
purpose in relationship to the sonnet or within itself. Yet the
first four lines have precision, dignity, and simplicity, which are
moving, and the twelfth line has subdued grandeur, due in part
to the heavy inversion of the third foot and to the heavy anapest
and iamb following. The high reputation of the sonnet is due
about equally, I suspect, to its virtues and its faults.

One of the most perplexing of the sonnets is CVII:

> Not mine own fears, nor the prophetic soul
> Of the wide world, dreaming on things to come,
> Can yet the lease of my true love control,
> Supposed as forfeit to a confin'd doom.
> The mortal moon hath her eclipse endured,
> And the sad augurs mock their own presage;
> Incertitudes now crown themselves assured,
> And peace proclaims olives of endless age.
> Now with the drops of this most balmy time
> My love looks fresh, and death to me subscribes,
> Since, spite of him, I'll live in this poor rime,
> While he insults o'er dull and speechless tribes:
> > And thou in this shalt find thy monument
> > When tyrants' crests and tombs of brass are spent.

The sonnet has given rise to a great deal of scholarly speculation,
most of which the reader can find summarized in Rollins's
variorum edition of the sonnets. One of the commonest interpre-
tations is that which identifies the mortal moon with Elizabeth
and the eclipse with her death. The friend, then, is Southampton, who was released from prison upon the accession of James,

and lines six, seven, eight, nine, and ten refer to the general fears that there would be civil disorder upon the death of Elizabeth and to the fact that James was nevertheless crowned with no disorder. The interpretation is fairly plausible, though by no means certain; but it involves two difficulties which, I think, have never been met. The tone of the poem is scarcely explained by this interpretation: the tone is sombre and mysterious, as if supernatural forces were under consideration—this tone is most obvious in the first quatrain, but it persists throughout. Furthermore, in line eleven we have a monstrous non sequitur, for there is not the remotest connection between Southampton's release from prison or the events leading up to it and Shakespeare's making himself and Southampton immortal in verse. To this objection the reader may reply that the concluding lines are merely in a Petrarchan convention and should not be taken too seriously. They may represent such a convention, but they have to be taken seriously, for the tone of seriousness and mystery, the magnificence of the language, are such that we are not prepared for triviality at this point. If this interpretation (or I think any other in the variorum editions) is accepted, then the poem stands as one of the most striking examples of Shakespeare's inability to control his language, of his tendency to indulge vague emotion with no respect for meaning. And the poem may, in fact, be such an example.

Leslie Hotson, however, has come forward with another theory.[2] He believes that the mortal moon (mortal: deadly, death-dealing) is the Spanish Armada, of which the line of battle was moon shaped, and which attacked England and was defeated in 1588, a year of which there had been dire predictions for

[2] *Shakespeare's Sonnets Dated, and other essays*, by Leslie Hotson (London, 1949).

generations, some of the prophets having thought it the year in which the world would end. Hotson is an irritating writer, as everyone who has read him carefully must know. But whatever objections one may have to Hotson's theory, there is no denying the fact that he documents it fully and impressively. Furthermore—and this is a point which Hotson fails to mention—this interpretation explains the mysterious tone of the poem (for in these terms we are dealing literally with supernatural forces, as well as with the most terrifying of natural forces), and it eliminates the non sequitur (for the lives of both the poet and the friend had been threatened, and both have survived). Hotson's theory clarifies the poem at every point, in spite of the conventional elements in the poem and the obscurely allusive manner of writing.

One can make certain obvious objections to Hotson's theory. For example, Hotson claims that the entire sequence was done by the age of twenty-five: this in spite of the facts that Shakespeare repeatedly refers to himself as an aging man and that there are many parallels in phrasing between the sonnets and the later plays. Furthermore, Hotson bases this claim on the explication of only one sonnet other than the sonnet just discussed. The management of the iambic pentameter line would seem to be too sensitive and skillful for a young man in 1588, although anything, of course, is possible when we are dealing with a poet of genius. But in favor of Hotson's view would be the very weaknesses which I have been describing—weaknesses which might well be those of a young man—although Hotson appears to be unaware of them. However, these weaknesses might easily be those of an older man, more at home in the dramatic form, writing carelessly for a private audience, and working in a style which in the course of his mature life became obsolete. Even with Hotson's explanation, however, or with another as good, the poem is faulty. No poem is wholly self-contained, but most poems work within frames of reference which are widely understood. This poem appears to have a very particular frame of reference about which it will always be impossible to be sure. The poem is almost all connotation, with almost no denotation; it is almost purely vehicle, with almost no tenor; it is almost wholly ornament, with almost nothing to which the ornament can be attached. It would be easy to say that such a poem is a kind of forerunner of some of the deliberately obscure work of the past hundred years; but this work is all based on closely related theories—those of Mallarmé or of Pound, for examples—and Shakespeare had no such theories. Shakespeare's ideas about the nature of poetry were those of his age, but he was often unable to write in accordance with them. Such a poem as this must have been the result of inadvertence.

Whatever the faults of the sonnets as wholes, their incidental beauties are numerous. These beauties are often of the most elusive kind, and they are probably felt by many readers without ever being identified. Consider, for example, line six of Sonnet XIX:

> And do Whate'er thou wilt, swift-footed Time.

There is a plaintive desperation in the line which it is impossible to describe but which any sensitive reader can feel. In what is being said there is a stereotyped but real and timeless fear, and this is expressed in part by the helplessness of the imperative and in part by the archaic cliché *swift-footed*. It is expressed also in the emphases of the rhythmical pattern: the first three feet are all heavily accented, but each succeeding foot more heavily than the one preceding, so that we reach a climax on *wilt*, followed by the long pause of the comma, the pause in turn followed by a foot lighter and more evenly stressed, and this by a very heavily stressed foot. This is not an original line nor a great one; it is derivative and minor—but it is moving.

More obvious are the moral perceptions in the second quatrain of XXIX:

> When in disgrace with fortune and men's eyes
> I all alone beweep my outcast state,
> And trouble deaf heaven with my bootless cries,
> And look upon myself, and curse my fate,
> Wishing me like to one more rich in hope,
> Featur'd like him, like him with friends possessed,
> Desiring this man's art, and that man's scope,
> With what I most enjoy contented least;
> Yet in these thoughts myself almost despising,
> Haply I think on thee,—and then my state,
> Like to the lark at break of day arising
> From sullen earth, sings hymns at heaven's gate;
>> For thy sweet love remember'd such wealth brings
>> That then I scorn to change my state with kings.

The first quatrain of this sonnet is a passable example of what the French would call *la poésie larmoyante*; it is facile melancholy at its worst. And yet the next four lines are precise and admirable; they are a fine example of the plain style. In the third quatrain we have the lark which has made the sonnet famous. The lark is an ornament, in the same way as Donne's compasses. In the last six lines we are told, of course, that the poet's state of mind has changed; and we are told why—he has thought of the friend or lady, whichever it may be. But this a sentimental, an almost automatic, change, and it is hard to understand after the four lines preceding. It is what I have previously called an evasion of the issue posed. And the lark is a sentimental lark: at the descriptive level, *sullen, sings hymns,* and *heaven's gate* are all inaccurate. The lark is burdened with the unexplained emotions of the poet. But the lark is not representative of any explanatory idea. The lark suffers in these ways from comparison with the pigeons of Wallace Stevens, of which I shall write briefly at the end of this essay. We have more lark than understanding in these lines, and more easy sentiment than lark.

One of the most fascinating passages is the description of the imperceptible but continuous action of Time in CIV:

> Ah! yet doth beauty like a dial hand
> Steal from his figure, and no pace perceived;
> So your sweet hue, which methinks still doth stand,
> Hath motion, and mine eye may be deceived.

And yet even here we are in grammatical difficulty, for it is the dial hand (or its shadow) which should steal from the figure; it is not beauty. Or if we take *figure* to mean the human form or face, then the dial hand is left with no reference, and there is no basis for the second half of the comparison. We understand the passage, of course, but the statement is careless.

One can find good poems among the sonnets which do not achieve at any point the greatness of certain lines from sonnets which fail. Such, for examples, are XXIII, CXXIX, and CXLVI. The first of these is correct but minor; the second ("The expense of spirit") is powerful in phrasing, but repetitious in structure—as Douglas Peterson has shown (*Shakespeare Quarterly* V-4), it derives its structure and much of its matter from a passage in Wilson's *Art of Rhetorique*—and appears to be a forceful exercise on a limited topic; the third is somewhat commonplace when compared with the best of Donne's *Holy Sonnets*.

The most impressive sonnet of all, I suspect, is LXXVII, in which the peculiarly Shakespearian qualities are put to good use, in which the peculiar faults are somehow transformed into virtues. Jonson, Donne, and Greville—indeed most of the great poets of the Renaissance—tend to deal with the experiential import of explicit definitions and sometimes to offer explicit and figurative excursions from definitions. In the plain style at its plainest, the passion with which the human significance of the definitions is felt is communicated by the emotional content of the language in which they are stated: that is, we do not have definition here and emotion there, but meaning and emotion coexist at every moment; in the relatively ornate style, the excursions are controlled in a general but clear way by the definitions. But Shakespeare's approach to his subject is indirect and evasive. In LXXVII the explicit subject is not very important: it provides the occasion for the entry into the poem of certain perceptions which appear to be almost accidental but which are really Shakespeare's obsessive themes.

LXXVII appears to have been written to accompany the gift of a blank book:

> Thy glass will show thee how thy beauties wear;
> Thy dial how thy precious minutes waste;
> The vacant leaves thy mind's imprint will bear,
> And of this book this learning may'st thou taste.
> The wrinkles which thy glass will truly show
> Of mouthed graves will give thee memory;
> Thou by thy dial's shady stealth may know
> Time's thievish progress to eternity.
> Look! what thy memory cannot contain
> Commit to these waste blanks, and thou shalt find
> Those children nursed, delivered from thy brain
> To take a new acquaintance of thy mind.

> These offices, so oft as thou wilt look,
> Shall profit thee and much enrich thy book.

The first quatrain states the ostensible theme of the poem: time passes and we age, yet by writing down our thoughts, we take a new acquaintance of our mind, acquire a new learning. The second quatrain enlarges upon the passage of time; the last six lines revert to the moralizing.

But something very strange occurs. The imperceptible coming of wrinkles displays the physical invasion of the enemy, just as the imperceptible movement of the dial's shadow displays the constant movement of the enemy. In the ninth line, however, the enemy invades the mind, the center of being; it was the figure of the book which enabled the poet to extend the poem to this brilliant and terrifying suggestion, yet so far as the development of the theme is concerned, the extension occurs almost by the way, as if it were a casual and merely incidental feeling.

> Look! What thy memory cannot contain
> Commit to these waste blanks . . . .

This command, in isolation, is merely a command to make good use of the book, and the remainder of the passage deals wholly with the advantages of doing so; yet the command follows the lines in which we have observed the destruction of the physical being by time, and in this position it suggests the destruction of the mind itself. This terrifying subject, the loss of identity before the uncontrollable invasion of the impersonal, is no sooner suggested than it is dropped.

There is a related but more curious employment of pure suggestion in the word *waste* in the same passage. The word is obviously a pun, with the emphasis on the secondary meaning.

It means not only *unused* or *blank* (this is the primary meaning, and it gives us a tautology), but it means *desert* or *uninhabited* or *uninhabitable*, a sense reinforced by the verb *waste* in the second line; but rationally considered, the pages are not waste in this second sense, but are instruments offered for actually checking the invasion of the waste. A feeling, in other words, is carried over from its proper motive to something irrelevant to it, and the dominant feeling is thus reinforced at the expense of the lesser; this dominant feeling, one should add, arises not from the ostensible theme of the poem—the book and its use—but from the incidental theme which has slipped into the poem. In order to express the invasion of confusion, the poem for a moment actually enters the realm of confusion instead of describing it. The poem, I think, succeeds; but after having examined the unsuccessful confusion of other sonnets, I cannot decide whether the success is due to skill or to accident.

III

The style of Ben Jonson is plain, but it is also urbane and polished. It has the solid structure of the styles of Gascoigne and Raleigh, with evidence of a knowledge of the flexibility of Sidney. Jonson is no such enraptured rhetorician as Sidney, but on the other hand his understanding of Sidneyan rhetoric prevents his indulging in any such affectation of roughness as we find to some extent in Gascoigne; he is freer from mannerism and a purer stylist than either, and, since he operates from a central position, he is more sensitive and more skillful than either, for he can employ the tones of both without committing himself wholly to one direction. Shakespeare, in comparison, succumbed to excessive and uncontrolled sensitivity; Donne shows the vices of both Gascoigne and Sidney, the affectation of harshness on the one hand and of sophisticated ingenuity on the other. Greville alone of this group rivals Jonson in control of his style and may surpass him in the range of his materials and the profundity of his thought; yet Jonson's style is more varied than Greville's and places him as the first master stylist of the plain tradition: that is to say, of the great tradition.

Jonson is a classicist in the best sense, and though his classicism is no doubt in part the result of his study of the Greek and Latin poets, critics, and rhetoricians, as it was probably in greater part the result of his natural bent, it is reasonable to see in his work a resolution of the qualities to be found in Sidney and the poets of the plain style. One does not learn to write English verse from studying Latin verse, though one may thus acquire applicable theories. Jonson must have been familiar with the poets whom I have mentioned; and these and a few others *were the English language*, so far as poetic style was concerned, at the time when Jonson was mastering the language, and there was little to distract the attention from them.

Like most of the lyrics of the period, Jonson's are expository in structure; but, unlike many, they engage in very little figurative excursion (such as one gets in Donne) and very little illustrative repetition (such as one gets in Nashe's " In Time of Pestilence "). They are very closely written arguments, or at least a good many of them are, and they have to be read very closely if one is not to lose the continuity of the arguments. He wrote a little devotional poetry of a high order, but his subject matter is chiefly ethical in the narrowest sense: that is, he deals with problems of conduct arising between one human being and another, or between one human being and the social group, or between one human being and other serious problems; indeed, his devotional poetry concerns itself explicitly with man's moral relationship with God. The language is accurate and concise with regard to both idea and feeling; there is an exact correlation between motive and feeling which may easily be mistaken for coldness and mechanical indifference by the reader accustomed to more florid enticements, but which impresses the present reader rather as integrity and nobility. Among Jonson's greatest poems illustrating these qualities are the following: "Though beauty be the mark of praise"; "Where dost thou careless lie"; "High-spirited friend"; "From death and dark oblivion near the same"; "False world, good night"; "Good and great God, can I not think of Thee"; "Let it not your wonder move"; and "To draw no envy, Shakespeare, on thy name."

I will begin with "An Elegy":

> Though beauty be the mark of praise,
>   And yours of whom I sing be such
>   As not the world can praise too much,
> Yet is't your virtue now I raise.
>
> A virtue like allay, so gone
>   Throughout your form, as though that move,
>   And draw and conquer all men's love,
> This subjects you to love of one.
>
> Wherein you triumph yet: because
>   'Tis of yourself, and that you use
>   The noblest freedom, not to choose
> Against or faith, or honor's laws.
>
> But who should less expect of you,
>   In whom alone love lives again?
>   By whom he is restored to men,
> And kept, and bred, and brought up true?
>
> His falling temples you have reared,
>   The withered garlands tane away;

His altars kept from the decay
That envy wished, and nature feared.

And on them burn so chaste a flame
  With so much loyalty's expense
  As love, t'acquit such excellence,
Is gone himself into your name.

And you are he: the Deity
  To whom all lovers are designed,
  That would their better objects find:
Among which faithful troup am I.

Who as an off'ring at your shrine,
  Have sung this hymn, and here entreat
  One spark of your diviner heat
To light upon a love of mine.

Which if it kindle not, but scant
  Appear, and that to shortest view,
  Yet give me leave t'adore in you
What I, in her, am grieved to want.

This is a poem in praise of a woman who is a friend, not the
beloved; she is praised for her virtue and her constancy in love,
at the expense of the woman whom the poet loves; and because
of these qualities she is identified with the god of love. The
theme is serious, and it is worked out in greater detail than my
summary would suggest. On the other hand, the theme is in no
wise difficult to understand, in spite of the compactness of the
writing.

The poem is far from simple, however, and much of it may
escape the reader who has read it for its paraphrasable content
alone. It is a fusion of two kinds of poetry: the song and the
didactic poem. It is a poem in praise of virtue in love; and, in
connection with love, the machinery of the old Religion of Love
(in which virtue as here conceived was scarcely an element) is

employed discreetly. The stanza frequently suggests a song stanza as it opens, and then seems to stop the song with a didactic close, as if strings had been plucked and then muted; and this effect, more or less inherent in the form of the stanza itself, is sometimes stressed and sometimes softened. In the first stanza, for example, the effect of the single-hearted love song is suggested in the first three lines, but qualified by *though* and by the harsh rimes *such* and *much*; and in the fourth line the tone is brought down firmly to the didactic. The second stanza suggests a song-movement throughout, and the subject of love in the second and third lines reinforces the movement; but the treatment of the subject is moralistic, and the song quality is softened by this fact. The third stanza is one of the most explicitly moralistic, yet the first clause suggests another tone, that of the triumphant love song; and this tone dominates the first three lines of the fourth stanza and is only partly muted in the fourth line. The fifth stanza resembles the fourth, but here the Religion of Love, which has been introduced quietly in the fourth, emerges strongly; and in the first two lines especially the accented syllables are heavy and long, and the unaccented are light, in such a way as to suggest a triumphal chant. In the remainder of the poem the didactic tone dominates, but it has already been so qualified by the other that the echo of the song is present most of the time, most plainly, perhaps, in the eighth stanza and most muted in the last.

It is all but impossible to describe the nuances of feeling which I have been trying to describe. The reader who comes to this poem must have a reasonably full acquaintance with the Elizabethan songs and with the tradition of the plain style; he must understand metrical structure and the various methods of rhythmic variation; and he must read carefully. There is nothing wasted in this poem. Every word is necessary to the argument; every cadence, every suggestion of literary tradition, whether that suggestion occur in the cadence or in the explicit meaning of the words, contributes to the feeling which the argument endeavors to convey; and the theme, though not the greatest conceivable, is a great one.

The language of the poem is essentially abstract, but it is worth our trouble to examine briefly the few references to concrete details. In the first stanza, *mark*, as I understand it, is a target, but we are not expected to visualize a target or shooting at a target or the raising of a target. The terms have receded into almost pure abstraction. In the second stanza, *allay* is, if this is possible, even closer to pure abstraction. The third and fourth stanzas are purely abstract. In the remainder of the poem, *temples, garlands, altars, flame, shrine, spark,* and *kindle* come a little closer to visibility, but the degree of visibility is small and the degree of abstraction is great. If these details were visualized more sharply, they would obstruct the argument, and the poem would be weakened further by the fact that these images, merely as images, would be stereotyped. The argument, however, is not stereotyped, but is original and moving, and these details do not obstruct: rather, they contribute to the feeling communicated by the argument by way of their connotations.

" To Heaven " is a greater poem. For one thing, the subject is greater. For another, the poem depends less heavily upon an antecedent body of poetry; and, although it depends upon an understanding of the Christian religious experience, this is more generally understood, and the poem moves more rapidly and with greater weight of meaning line by line. In other words, the poem is more nearly self-contained.

Good and great God, can I not think of Thee,
But it must, straight, my melancholy be?
Is it interpreted in me disease,
That, laden with my sins, I seek for ease?
O be Thou witness, that the reins dost know
And hearts of all, if I be sad for show;
And judge me after: if I dare pretend
To aught but grace, or aim at other end.
As Thou art all, so be Thou all to me,
First, midst, and last, converted One and Three!
My faith, my hope, my love; and in this state,
My judge, my witness, and my advocate.
Where have I been this while exiled from Thee,
And whither rap'd, now Thou but stoop'st to me?
Dwell, dwell here still! O, being everywhere,
How can I doubt to find Thee ever here?
I know my state, both full of shame and scorn,
Conceived in sin, and unto labor born,
Standing with fear, and must with horror fall,
And destined unto judgment after all.
I feel my griefs too, and there scarce is ground
Upon my flesh t'inflict another wound:
Yet dare I not complain or wish for death,
With holy Paul, lest it be thought the breath
Of discontent; or that these prayers be
For weariness of life, not love of Thee.

This poem deals with a major theme, and there are no crude flaws; yet this could be true and the poem still fall short of mastery. The reasons for the success of the poem are hard to describe, for there is no imagery, no decoration, and the metrical and stanzaic forms employed are the simplest in English. The poem has no faults that I can discover, and faults are always easier to discuss than virtues. The surface is tight and smooth; there is almost no opening.

Yet one can note certain facts, at the risk, perhaps, of seeming pedantic. The rhythmic structure of the line is of the post-Sidneyan variety: that is, the accented syllables (and the unaccented also) vary widely in degree of accentuation, so that the line is flexible and subtle, rather than heavy and emphatic. The cesuras are managed with great skill: they fall most often after the second foot or the third, or in the middle of the third, but in line twenty the cesura falls in the middle of the fourth foot; and in many lines the secondary pauses complicate the cesural structure greatly, for example, in ten, eleven, and twelve, and there are other less obvious examples. The heroic couplet is used in these respects with a skill that one can seldom find equalled within similar limits by Dryden or Pope. The relationship of sentence structure to linear and stanzaic structure is similarly brillant: the closed couplet is the norm, and the first, second, seventh, and eighth couplets are complete units, the last of these containing two closely related sentences, the others one each; the third and fourth couplets, the fifth and sixth, the ninth and tenth, the eleventh and twelfth and thirteenth, are longer units; and within these sentences there is considerable variety of structure regardless of length, this variety affecting not merely the sentence but the rhythm of the line and of the group of lines.

Jonson employs two other common devices in this poem: the play upon words in the eighth couplet (*everywhere* and *ever here*), and the play upon an idea (that of the Trinity) in the fifth and sixth couplets. This kind of ingenuity resulted in some of the best and some of the worst passages in the Renaissance; the ingenuity here seems not only justifiable but inescapable: it is an essential part of the argument.

The series of triads resulting from the concept of the Trinity is especially impressive: it occurs in brief space and rapidly; it is not forced but seems a natural series of comparisons; it speeds the rhythm for a few lines (at a moment when the increased speed is a proper expression of passion); and it varies the rhythm of the whole poem, providing a fine preparation for the slower and more sombre movement of the later lines. It prepares us likewise for the final series of theological statements, which, however, are not arranged in triads—those in couplets nine and ten.

The devices which I have described are simple, when considered in general; their effectiveness, like the effectiveness of that other simple device, good diction, depends upon the fine shades in which they appear in the particular context—these fine shades are among the principal marks of genius. These fine shades of statement, however, could not exist were it not for the clear substance of the poem and the clear organization of the substance. In connection with this clarity—which may appear to some to be simplicity—there is one point which I think it worth while to bring surely to light: the theme of this poem is somewhat less simple than it may appear at first glance. The poem deals with love for God and the desire for death. God is perfect being, and therefore good; life, as the poet knows it, is being, however imperfect, and therefore good as a matter of theory. But Jonson, in middle age, does not fear death, as Shakespeare professes to fear it and as Donne apparently fears it in fact: his temptation is " weariness of life "; his duty, which he accepts with a semi-suppressed despair, is to overcome this weariness. There is a recognition of reality here, distinct from a literary convention (as in Shakespeare) and from a gift for personal drama, or perhaps melodrama (as in Donne), which is very impressive. Much of the power of the poem resides in one of the elementary facts of life: the fact that a middle-aged man of intelligence is often readier to die than to live if he merely indulges his feelings. Jonson deals with the real problem, not with a spurious problem.

These two poems illustrate the qualities which I have been trying to describe; they illustrate a plainness more akin to Gascoigne or Wyatt, or especially to Greville, than to any obvious quality in Sidney; Jonson, like Greville, is one on whom the black ox has trod. But these poems illustrate especially that fine control of nuances of feeling which are possible only to the stylist who deliberately abandons, yet remembers, the obvious graces; such writing is not only more weighty than that of Sidney, but it is more sensitive, more skillful.

Jonson's major poems have been neglected in favor of his minor poems, masterly performances in themselves, but less illustrative both of Jonson's genius and the age. The minor poems carry something over from the old courtly tradition to the new: the courtly element is offered playfully in Jonson and in his disciples of the seventeenth century; it is not offered with the benumbing pretence of seriousness which we find in Sidney and Spenser and others. The minor lyrics, however, with the aid of his plays, other writings, and legendary personality, have been able to keep him in some measure before the student's eye as a lyrical poet; he has never, in this capacity, lapsed into the obscurity in which Raleigh was long permitted to rest and in which Gascoigne and Greville rest to this day. If the reader with fixed habits could wrench his attention to the major poems long enough to appreciate them, this act would not only put him in possession of what is probably one of the two or three greatest bodies of short poems composed in the English Renaissance but would aid him to understand a number of other great poets as well.

Among the lesser of Jonson's poems which should be read

with especial care are these: the epitaphs on his children, especially that on his son; the epitaph on Salathiel (or Salomon) Pavy; "This morning timely rapt with holy fire" (to the Countess of Bedford); "A Hymn to God the Father"; the second poem to Charis; "The Hour Glass"; "My Picture Left in Scotland"; and the song in *Love's Triumph through Callipolis* beginning: "Joy, joy to mortals the rejoicing fires." There are in addition the justly famous minor masterpieces such as "Drink to me only with thine eyes," and "Queen and huntress chaste and fair," poems which discipline the heritage of the song books and bequeath it to the seventeenth century.

IV

During the Renaissance, the style of the short poem is largely classifiable as ornate or plain, although both elements may occur in one poem. When sensory detail is employed, it is commonly in the form of ornament. In certain poems the ornate style is controlled with a good deal of firmness, but the sensory detail is nevertheless ornament, something added, something attached. The poems of the plain style, however, concentrate on the essential theme, and the best of them seem to me the best poems of the period.

But the plain style sacrifices a part of our experience, the sensory, and the ornate style does not really recover it in a satisfactory way. We are, of course, rational animals, and most of our thinking is done in abstractions, and this was going on even before Plato; and we have become familiar with abstractions and with their relationships to daily experience—they can be used with emotional force as well as with intellectual. But we are also sensory animals, and we live in a physical universe, and if we are blind to the impressiveness and meanings of our physical surroundings, we are limited. It ought to be possible to embody our sensory experience in our poetry in an efficient way, not as ornament, and with no sacrifice of rational intelligence.

In the eighteenth century, poets and theorists of poetry, harking back to Hobbes and Locke, decided that all ideas arise from the association of sense-perceptions. By the end of the century it was often believed that ideas could be expressed in terms of sense-perceptions. This notion is foolish: no matter how ideas may have arisen, they cannot at this late date be equated with the impressions of sense. The notion is, however, precisely the basis of Pound's theory of the image and of the ideogram, and is the central idea in most of the Romantic theories of poetry in the United States, England, France, and other Western countries in the nineteenth and twentieth centuries. Since ideas cannot really be expressed purely in terms of sense-perceptions, we are merely given pure sense-perceptions. We get what Frank Kermode has called the romantic image—that is, the mindless image, the impenetrable image, which seems to mean but in reality merely is.[3] Mallarmé's poetic absolute is a version of this idea. Most of our contemporary poets and critics are operating on one form or another of it. The associationists provided another principle, however—one of structure: instead of the rational structure of the Renaissance, we were offered a structure based on association. Most of Pound's *Cantos* illustrate both of these principles in an extreme form, and in spite of the talent which went into this lifelong experiment, they are far from satisfactory. However, it is possible to employ associative structure without sensory imagery: one finds it in much of the work of Charles Churchill.

[3] *Romantic Image* (Macmillan, New York, 1957).

It is possible also to keep both of these principles under sufficiently strict control to make them very useful, to make them, in fact, means to enrich the older procedures.

I have already published a brief discussion of controlled associationism in connection with Paul Valéry.[4] I will now say a few words about it as we find it in Stevens's " Sunday Morning." However, where the principles of structure and of imagery are both involved, I think that we have controlled associationism primarily in the structure. The imagery is post-associationistic. Let us call the total method post-symbolist.

Stevens, in his best poems, is a master of the resources of meter and syntax, and of the resources of rhythm that can result from meter and syntax; and he is a master of diction. These facts are well known, and I shall waste no time on them; but I would like to add that in my opinion he is, in these respects, fully the equal of Ben Jonson and the superior of Donne, Sidney, or the Shakespeare of the sonnets. What I would like to discuss briefly is the nature and function of his imagery.

" Sunday Morning " deals primarily with a doctrine that one can call Paterian hedonism. I have objected to this doctrine elsewhere, and I will not repeat myself. The poem deals also with the rejection of Christianity and with the imminence of death in a universe which is at once infinitely beautiful and perfectly incomprehensible. It is with this view of the universe and with certain aspects of man's place in it, as the imagery is used to express this view, that I am now concerned, and I shall discuss only a few passages of the poem.

In the first stanza the protagonist

---

[4] *The Function of Criticism: Problems and Exercises* (Alan Swallow, Denver, 1957), pp. 58–75.

> . . . feels the dark
> Encroachment of that old catastrophe,
> As a calm darkens among water-lights.

The catastrophe I take to be death in general and the death of Jesus in particular. If one has ever seen a calm darken among water lights on a large bay or lake, the image is unforgettable. A few lines farther on, "The day is like wide water without sound," and the water image is extended. In the next six stanzas the religious and ethical problems are discussed, and then in the final stanza we return to the water, which by now has become more real than figurative:

> She hears upon that water without sound,
> A voice that cries, "The tomb in Palestine
> Is not the porch of spirits lingering.
> It is the grave of Jesus, where he lay."

And then:

> We live in an old chaos of the sun,
> Or old dependency of day and night,
> Or island solitude, unsponsored, free,
> Of that wide water, inescapable.

In the first water image, death encroached as a calm darkens among water lights; then the day was like water; then infinite space is water—bright, beautiful, and inscrutable, the home of life and death. Every phrase in this last passage is beautiful at the descriptive level, but the descriptive and the philosophical cannot be separated: *chaos, solitude, unsponsored, free, inescapable* work at both levels. The sensory detail is not ornament; it is a part of the essential theme. In the next three lines there is a measure of separation:

> Deer walk upon our mountains, and the quail

> Whistle about us their spontaneous cries;
> Sweet berries ripen in the wilderness;

Out of context, this is merely description, but fine description. In context, it is a part of what precedes and what follows, but there is only one word which makes a philosophical connection: *spontaneous*. The quail are nonhuman, free, spontaneous: they can be admired but not understood; they are part of the wilderness. The last lines are similar, except that the number of charged words is greater:

> And, in the isolation of the sky,
> At evening, casual flocks of pigeons make
> Ambiguous undulations as they sink
> Downward to darkness on extended wings.

Out of context, these lines are fine description but minor poetry; in context, they are great poetry, and the words responsible are: *isolation, casual, ambiguous,* and *darkness.* Out of context, these words would not be suspected, I imagine, of carrying any real weight of meaning beyond the descriptive meaning. Their significance has been prepared by the total poem, and they sum the poem up.

These pigeons are different from Shakespeare's lark. The lark was merely a lark, with the author's personal sentimentality imposed upon it arbitrarily. The pigeons embody an idea as well as a feeling, and the idea motivates the feeling. The pigeons cannot be separated from the idea: they are a part of the universe which the poet is trying to understand, and at this point they are an efficiently representative part. The rational soul and the sensible soul are united: we do not have the purely rational soul of Jonson or the purely sensible soul of Pound; and there is no decoration. The universe which Stevens describes is ambiguous in its ultimate meanings, but there is nothing ambiguous in the style: ambiguity is rendered with the greatest of precision. And the universe is one which we can recognize as our own, even if we disagree with Stevens's philosophy. The physical details are not ingenious set pieces; we know where we are.

There is more to the art of poetry than a kind of imagery or the lack of imagery. As I have said, we must have an important theme, an understanding of the theme which is in some measure defensible, and a command of syntax, meter, rhythm, and diction; and one will not come by these simple-sounding acquisitions without both genius and education. But the post-symbolist sensibility, other things being equal, seems to me potentially the greatest achievement in occidental poetry. One can find examples of it earlier: in Emily Dickinson and F. G. Tuckerman, and occasionally, perhaps, in Baudelaire and in Leconte de Lisle; but it emerges most clearly in Valéry and Stevens. I doubt that either of these men understood the implications of the style of his best work. Neither was a scholar, and the theoretical statements of both are confused. Both were caught in an historical movement which they understood imperfectly. But they had sufficient genius to make the most of their immediate background in a few poems. The poems are there to be understood, and if we can understand them, we may well be at the beginning of the greatest poetical movement that we have known.

Marianne Moore

Dame

Edith

Sitwell

GREAT IN FAR GREATER WAYS, DAME Edith Sitwell is a virtuoso of rhythm and accent. She has given me immense pleasure, intensifying my interest in rhythm, and has also encouraged me in my rhythmic eccentricities. I can scarcely read the Bible without forsaking content for rhythm, as where the Apostle Paul speaks of the shipwreck on Malta and says, " when the ship could no longer bear up into the wind, we let her drive." "Let her drive" is a better rhythm, is it not, than we have in the new version, which reads "and were driven?" "When we could not face the wind, we gave way to it and were driven."

Façade was apprenticeship, Dame Edith, or Miss Sitwell as she was then, insists, but an apprenticeship of great virtuosity; and of wit as in "The Higher Sensualism" when Queen Circe said

> " Young man, I will buy
> Your plumaged coat for my pig to try—
>
> Then with angels he'll go a-dancing hence
> From sensuality into sense! "

"I used to practice writing," Dame Edith says, "as a pianist practices music." She says that she would take a waltz or a polka or the music of the barrel organ beneath her window and translate it into words, just as she has done in the phrase from this "Country Dance."

> But Silenus
> Has seen us.

Dame Edith then explored the nature of the long line and its possibilities. William Carlos Williams has said in his book *I Wanted to Write a Poem*, "I found I could not use the long line because of my nervous nature." An adagio, moreover, "is hard to sustain at concert pitch," as *The Times Literary Supplement* has said. We have it, however, when Edith Sitwell writes

> archipelagoes
> Of stars and young thin moons from great wings falling
> As ripples widen.

How pleasing, her dactyls: *porphyry, basicilica, Babylyn*; and *babioun* (*babioun* borrowed from Ben Jonson, as she says). How neat, the rhyme "Noctambulo" with "folio":

> The public scribe, Noctambulo
> Where moonlight, cold as blades of grass
> Echoes upon deserted walls,
> Turned his dusty folio;

and this: "old Bacchantes black with wine, / Whose very hair has changed into a vine." We have here, I think, something of the automatic self-initiated effect of Leslie Brooke's "Johnny Crow's Party":

> The snake
> Got entangled
> With the rake.

> The sheep
> Fell asleep
> And the armadillo
> Used him as a pillow.

Dame Edith's irregularities in set meter are hyper-skilful, as when she creates a pause after *any* in " anybody "—in " Mary Stuart to James Bothwell " (Casket Letter No. 2):

> Leaving you, I was sundered like the sea!
> Departed from the place where I left my heart
> I was as small as any body may be.

That is to say, any *body*, with the accent on body.

There is no melody in Pope, Dame Edith says, because there is no irregularity. " To have melody, there must be variations in the outward structure." An expert of the condensed phrase, she also says, " I try to make my images exact "; and does she not as in the word " sundered " and by inventing " donkey's hide-grass " for the beast of the attorney?

> O'er donkey's hide-grass the attorney
> Still continues on his journey.

In the opening lines of " The Sleeping Beauty," the incantatory effect of the whole passage is a metaphor creating a sense, I think, of deep, mysterious, fairyworld remoteness:

> When we come to that dark house,
> Never sound of wave shall rouse
> The bird that sings within the blood
> Of those who sleep in that deep wood.

Dame Edith reminds Katherine Anne Porter of Lully, Rameau, Monteverdi, and Purcell, of old courtly music, weddings, christenings, great crystal-lighted banquets, in sweet-smelling gardens under the full moon. Generalizing, she says, "There is no finer sight than to see an artist growing great." Sir George Sitwell, Dame Edith's father, said, "Edith will commit suicide when she finds she cannot write poetry." A need for this has not arisen.

One cannot, of course, exhibit virtuosity without being deplored and combatted. As Mr. Henry McBride—art critic for *The Dial*, the New York *Sun*, and *The Art News*—has said, "One may judge the vitality of an artist by the extent to which he is resisted." Dame Edith recalls that certain lines of hers once received "a mingling of bouquets and brickbats—with a strong predominance of brickbats"; yet invariably, as *The New Statesman and Nation* said on June 23, 1954, "losing every battle, she won the campaign"; in fact, "emerged more majestic, more unaccountably modern than ever."

In *Façade* she said that it was necessary to find heightened expression for the heightened speed of our time. However, she added "in spite of the fact that the rhythms which I practised in *Façade* were heightened, concentrated, and frequently more violent than those of the poets who had preceded us immediately, it was supposed by many that I had *discarded* rhythm. But we must not complain if the patterns in our mundane works are not perceived by the unobservant," this allusion being to Bishop Burnet, who had found fault with the constellations and said, if only the stars had been composed "according to the rules of art and symmetry."

Some readers may regard a word of Dame Edith's as arbitrary, or a statement may be termed "a shade oracular." In her choice of words, she is to herself always justified. "Neatness of execution is essential to sublimity," she says; and she indeed improves DeQuincey when she considers language an "incarnation" of thought rather than "the dress of thought." She is instructively "neat" in revising her own work; in substitutions, for instance, of a general term for a specific in her "Metamorphosis."

> When first the dew with golden foot
> Makes tremble every leaf and strawberry root.

This is made to read in the second version of 1946:

> Here once in Spring, the dew with golden foot
> Made tremble every leaf and hidden root.

When she exhibits other authors—Christopher Smart, for instance, in her early three volume anthology, and when in *The Book of the Winter* she selects examples from Herrick, Blake, and Donne—her wand is tipped with a diamond. Of compiling *The Book of the Winter*, Dame Edith said, "I was not concerned with producing a hodge-podge of everything that has been written about winter. . . . One of the greatest difficulties encountered in making an anthology of this kind is to resign oneself to omissions. I have had to exclude many beauties because they pulled the pattern out of shape." From Donne, it is not complementary spectacular matched lines of verse which she quoted, but this passage from a sermon preached by Donne in April, 1629: "The root of all is God, but it is not the way to receive fruits to dig at the root but to reach to the boughs." For Dylan Thomas, we have this all-encompassing apologia: "His love for those who have received no mercies from life is great." *The Book of the Winter* is marked by fire and novelty throughout, as in Sir Thomas Browne's "Of Crystals and Icicles"; and in this apparition or vision from *I Live under a Black Sun*— Dame Edith's novel: "A figure would shine through the night, circling swiftly as if it were a swallow, or floating, a black swan on the wide water-black marble pavements; . . . Rag Castle after rag castle, the world of beggars was swept along, and night fell upon the two nations, the rich and the poor, who alone inhabit the earth." Here are prototypes of Lazarus and Dives, made so emphatic in Dame Sitwell's later work. Tom O' Bedlam (anonymous), quoted only in part, perhaps epitomizes the contagion of the whole book:

> While I do sing,
> " Any food, any feeding,
> Feeding, drink, or clothing,"
> Come dame or maid
> Be not afraid
> Poor Tom will injure nothing.
>
> The meek, the wise, the gentle
> Me handle, touch, and spare not;
> But those that cross
> Tom Rhinoceros
> Do what the panther dare not.
>
> .   .   .   .   .
>
> With an host of furious fancies,
> Whereof I am commander,
> With a burning Speare, and a horse of aire,
> To the wildernesse I wander.

In his Introduction to Paul Valéry's *The Art of Poetry*, T. S. Eliot says, seemingly as an afterthought, " How Poetry is related to life, Valéry does not say." My own thought here, may be at a tangent from the query which Mr. Eliot may imply; but for me there is immediacy in Edith Sitwell's statement: " The behaviour of the world affects our beliefs and incites the mind to tumult to speak as a Cassandra or as an elegist." Her " awareness of the potentialities of atomic research," as a press commentator has said, " make more emphatic her assurance of the spiritual power behind the material façade." Reflecting current thought—or so I hope—Robert Frost has simplified the matter

of why we write when he says, "It is what every poem is about—
how the spirit is to surmount the material pressure upon us."

In our battle with the material world, does not Edith Sitwell
rise to bear humanity aid? "As for the poet taking an interest in
his fellow human being," she says, "he is a brother speaking to
a brother . . . supporting his brother's flagging footsteps." Over-
powered by a sense of the Universal Cain, of brother as murderer
of brother, of the chaingang sentenced to ninety-nine years, she
says, "I come to testify." And of her testimony, W. B. Yeats
said, "Something absent from all literature was back again,
passion ennobled by intensity, by endurance, by wisdom."

> "With what are these on fire?" she asks, "with passion, Hate,
> Infatuation, and old age, and death
> With sorrow, longing, and with laboring breath."

Time (December 26, 1955) said, "she writes for the sake of
sound, of color, and from an awareness of God and regard for
man." She herself says, "All great poetry is dipped in the dyes
of the heart," and quoting perhaps from Whitman, "all things
are in the clime of man's forgiveness." As one thinks of her
poetry, who could lament, as the *London Times Literary Supplement* says certain poets do, "our lack of the large theme and
forcible expression of it?" "To what ideals would I reach in my
poetry?" Dame Edith asks. "How far I am from these no one
could see more clearly than I. Technically, I would come to a
vital language—each word possessing an infinite power of germi-
nation. Spiritually to give holiness to each common day." By
reason of her humility and her compassion—I would not qualify
it—she cages conviction.

Mark Van Doren

The Poems of

Thomas Hardy

A TEXT FOR ANY DISCUSSION OF Thomas Hardy's poems might be the 373rd Pensée of Pascal: "I shall here write my thoughts without order, and not perhaps in unintentional confusion; that is true order, which will always indicate my object by its very disorder. I should do too much honor to my subject if I treated it with order, since I want to show that it is incapable of it." Pascal's subject, to be sure, was not anybody's poems; it was everybody's life; it was the whole of experience as he tried to grasp it. Yet the text has a peculiar fitness in Hardy's case, for it can be made to refer not merely to the overwhelming volume and variety of his poetic output but to the view he himself took of the world; or the views, for there were many of these, and he never pretended that they were consistent with one another.

In one of his prefaces he confessed how difficult it had been to arrange the present poems in anything like a natural or rational order. Indeed, it was impossible, and so he had given up. "I mean," he said, "the chance little shocks that may be caused

83

. . . by the juxtaposition of unrelated, even discordant, effusions; poems perhaps years apart in the making, yet facing each other. . . . But the difficulties of arranging the themes in a graduated kinship of moods would have been so great that irrelation was almost unavoidable with efforts so diverse. I must trust for right note-catching to those finely-touched spirits who can divine without half a whisper, whose intuitiveness is proof against all the accidents of inconsequence." The problem, familiar of course to any poet, must have been particularly torturous for Hardy, who had been prolific for so long. The eight volumes of short poems he published between 1898 and 1928—between, that is, his fifty-eighth and his eighty-eighth years—contained by no means all new matter. He was always bringing forward poems he had written in the 1860's, or in any of the three subsequent decades; for he started as as poet, and only because he could not get published in that capacity had he written novels. Now that he was determined to be known as a poet and nothing but a poet he ransacked his desk for "effusions" that might still do. No wonder he found it difficult to arrange the result.

The modern reader cannot do so either; nor can the modern critic decide with readiness which poems of Hardy's are the best, let alone the most characteristic. No poet more stubbornly resists selection. And this has not been to Hardy's advantage in the field where reputations are made. There is no core of pieces, no inner set of classic or perfect poems, which would prove his rank. Perhaps no poem of Hardy's is perfect; indeed, there is no great poet in whom imperfection is easier to find. Yet he is a great poet, and there are those who love him without limit even though they will admit his thousand failures and defects. With such persons it is the whole of him that registers and counts; one thing they would be reluctant to admit, namely, that out of his *Collected Poems* a *Selected Poems* might be put together which would contain everything pertaining to his essence. His essence, they would insist, is everywhere in the body of his work: in the capillaries, the tissues, no less than in the sinews and the heart. For them, in other words, the *Collected Poems* is neither too long nor too miscellaneous; its reputation with them depends upon the very richness that puts other readers off. They have made the effort the volume requires, and the reward of that effort is their knowledge of a poet who is great even when he is not writing well. He is great in himself, as one who thinks, feels, sees, and speaks; and he cannot lose their allegiance.

This miracle is worked in the *Collected Poems* alone; not in the slight verse play, *The Famous Tragedy of the Queen of Cornwall*, nor even in that more impressive drama in one-hundred and thirty scenes, *The Dynasts*. It is good to have read *The Dynasts* once, for it contains curious and wonderful things; but few can have read it twice, at least all the way through. It does not get close to its people, whom Hardy too convincingly calls automata, cheese-mites, and mackerel. The view he takes of them is from too far away. This of course is the view he wants to take, since a theory rules him as he writes: a theory not unlike that of Tolstoy as he wrote *War and Peace* on the same subject, the wars of Napoleon. For neither man did individuals count, at any rate so far as theory went: there was no such thing as character or will, there was only mass movement, and even in this movement there was no meaning. But Tolstoy so far forgot his theory as to create Natasha, Andrey, and Pierre, to name only three out of dozens of souls to whom his pen gave life; whereas Hardy, with that stubbornness which his admirers will always forgive him, refused to budge from the platform he had

erected whereon to stand and state his thesis—the calamity of
Napoleon was fortuitous, without design or moral, nor were
the sufferings of innumerable men so much as noted by the
Immanent Will whose unfeeling mind worked

> unconsciously, as heretofore,
> Eternal artistries in Circumstance.

The Spirits with whom Hardy shares his platform, bodiless
beings who have no more control over the drama than he has,
say magnificent things in a monotone their poet never violates;
but they say what he chooses to have them say, since they are
nothing but spokesmen for his metaphysics. When we descend
into the action—battles, conferences, love passages, riots, and
duels—we do not find ourselves among people to whom warmth
has even by inadvertence been given. Nor do these people speak
fine verse, as often the Spirits do; they are not enough alive for
that, nor does Hardy wish them to be. He has been more eloquent in his stage-directions; it is to those that the reader is most
likely to return. For example, this early one:

> The nether sky opens, and Europe is disclosed as a prone
> and emaciated figure, the Alps shaping like a backbone, and
> the branching mountain-chains like ribs, the peninsular pla-
> teau of Spain forming a head. Broad and lengthy lowlands
> stretch from the north of France across Russia like a grey-
> green garment hemmed by the Ural mountains and the glis-
> tening Arctic Ocean.
>
> The point of view then sinks downward through space,
> and draws near to the surface of the perturbed countries,
> where the peoples, distressed by events which they did not
> cause, are seen writhing, heaving, and vibrating in their
> various cities and nationalities.

That is eloquent, surely; indeed, it is brilliant; but it closes a door on drama which is something like the door of a tomb. Those of us who insist on entering must abandon all hope of making human sense out of what we see.

No, it is the *Collected Poems* upon which Hardy's reputation will be obliged to rest. And this is a volume, as has already been hinted, in which a traveller can lose his way. Its contents are a cavern the quality of whose darkness is always changing, and the number of whose recesses appears to increase as the explorer stumbles on. Lights gleam and then subside, only to be lit again in further corners. The reader, that is to say, is forever making new discoveries: either of Hardy or of himself. If of Hardy, they have to do with dimensions of his thought and feeling not previously observed. If of himself, they have to do with certain poems he seems to be reading for the first time; or reading with a sense of power in them that startles him, for there had been no sign of it before. No poet has so changeable a surface as Hardy, no poet maintains in his reader so changeable a mind. Which are his best poems, and which are his worst? The question never seems to get settled; no wonder he becomes the anthologist's despair.

Hardy himself has been before us in the cavern, lighting candles that would seem to show the way. Only, they do not show it all. They show, in fact, only their own wicks and tallow. They are the "philosophical" poems in which Hardy states his theory of life. It is the same theory that he states in *The Dynasts*, and it is equally unilluminating of anything save his own conscious thought. They are good poems, but they are not the ones that move us to call him a great poet. We want more from a poet than a theory of life; we want, if such a thing is possible, the look, feel, sound, taste, and even smell of life itself. And that is what Hardy eventually provides, and provides so richly

that his name is sure to last. Meanwhile there are these philosophical poems which tell us that he finds no intelligibility in
events, no form or order in the world. They are such poems as
only he could write; they say what they have to say in his own
idiom, for he meant very personally what he said in them; and
they make a solemn, piercing music which alone would certify
their sincerity. But they are not the heart of the book as he
must have supposed they would be. They take their place among
the thinner tissues, the ones with the least blood in them.

The heart of the book, assuming it can be located at all, is
older and tougher than these poems are. The book was not a
single effort like *The Dynasts*, conceived and carried through
with little or no interruption; it was the work of almost seventy
years, and Hardy himself changed much in all that time. Or if
he did not change, he submitted himself to many chances, and
caught on the fly a bewildering number of perceptions which in
the nature of things could not have been alike. An assiduous
taker of notes upon himself, he rendered on a wide front his
experience of the world, so that there is scarcely anything he
has not understood and said before he is finished. This is not
precisely to say that the rest of the book contradicts or denies
the philosophical poems. Rather, it absorbs them; it finds a place
for them and leaves them there.

In that place they say the same thing over and over: nature
and man have come to a misunderstanding, and this misunderstanding will never be cured. Nature—sometimes the term is
God—did not make man to think and feel; man was once unconscious, as other things still are, as mildews and mandrakes
are, as stones and birds. That was the good time, when suffering
of course existed yet could not tell itself it did; when no creature
expected more than it could get; when the " disease of feeling "

and the malady of thought had not yet been born in the brain of one creature, man, who now is doomed to pain by the very fact of this monstrous birth. The qualities we think distinguish us are the qualities that make us miserable. We long for what we can never have, just as we agonize over losses and failures of which nature takes only routine account.

If we could be one with nature again, as Lucretius thought we could, and as Naturalism says we must, we might recover that happiness of which we were unconscious when we had it; but this can never be. The gulf between us and our maker widens with every idea we have, and with every refinement of experience. Nature remains the same; we change, and in the process move away from her into a loneliness for which there is no remedy. The more we use our minds, the less we understand; yet we must keep on using our minds, as we must keep on hoping and despairing. Even nature is aware of all this, and laments her wayward child; though the only thing she can tell us is that if we came back to her we would be coming back to unconsciousness, we would be as toads and stars, as mushrooms and meteors.

> Maybe now
> Normal unawareness waits rebirth.

So in his last book, *Winter Words*, Hardy dares to hope; but it is the dimmest hope, and of the dimmest thing.

No wonder Hardy calls himself a tragic poet, and says on one occasion: "Comedy lies." No wonder he is at home with gloom, which he certainly is; or that he can note as a scientist would some signs that the world, like any other machine, is running down. In an uncanny poem, "Nature's Questioning," he even endows inanimate objects with the power to wonder what men wonder:

When I look forth at dawning, pool,
    Field, flock, and lonely tree,
    All seem to gaze at me
Like chastened children sitting silent in a school;

   Their faces dulled, constrained, and worn,
    As though the master's ways
    Through the long teaching days
Had cowed them till their early zest was overborne.

   Upon them stirs in lippings mere
    (As if once clear in call,
    But now scarce breathed at all)—
"We wonder, ever wonder, why we find us here!

   "Has some vast Imbecility,
    Mighty to build and blend,
    But impotent to tend,
Framed us in jest, and left us now to hazardry?

   "Or come we of an Automaton
    Unconscious of our pains? . . .
    Or are we live remains
Of Godhead dying downwards, brain and eye now gone?"

These are terrible questions, put with a terrible candor, which
of course is Hardy's. There is one further question, more difficult for Hardy to phrase because it seems to him rhetorical:

   "Or is it that some high Plan betides,
    As yet not understood,
    Of Evil stormed by Good,
We the Forlorn Hope over which Achievement strides?"

He phrases it rather stuffily; he is not convinced that it was
worth asking; but then he closes with music—his music—on the
note most native to him:

   Thus things around. No answerer I . . .
    Meanwhile the winds, and rains,

> And Earth's old glooms and pains
> Are still the same, and Life and Death are neighbors nigh.

"Are still the same." Perhaps the heart of Hardy is just there. Winds and rains, and glooms and pains—those are the matter out of which he makes his art; they are the very folklore of his life, the familiar data, never to disappear, over which his imagination can pore without becoming tired. He would not know what to do without them; and once he said as much, in the poem he wrote refusing an invitation to the United States. Our claim to be young and happy was precisely what kept him away:

> I shrink to seek a modern coast
> Whose riper times have yet to be;
> Where the new regions claim them free
> From that long drip of human tears
> Which peoples old in tragedy
> Have left upon the centuried years.

No, he must remain where men, bent under pressures unimaginable in a new world, were all but deformed by pain and failure. His allegiance was to irony: to the monstrous coincidence, the ghastly event, or else—reducing calamity's scale—to the queer outcome, the miniature misadventure, the misery no bigger than a mouse. It was characteristic of Hardy that his poem about the sinking of the *Titanic* dealt with only one fact: the building of the iceberg and the building of the ship at whatever moment in each case would bring it about that the two collided when and where they did. But it was just as characteristic of him that he should write, in "The Sun on the Letter," about the odd circumstance that sunlight played as brightly over bad news as it would have over good. The size of things did not matter to him so long as all of them, huge or minute, testified to the principle of chance—or, as he put it in an early poem,

Hap. Crass Casualty was still another name for it. And in nature as men once knew her it would not have been noticed, since nothing would have been noticed. It is the disease of feeling that has made men hypersensitive to truth: they cannot take what must be and what is. They are skinless creatures, shivering in the winds of circumstance.

Now it might follow from the firmness with which Hardy held on to this view that he would have no sympathy with those who feel; that he would spend all of his strength, as Lucretius did, in lecturing them upon the absurdity of their error; that he would, in other words, be cold and heartless. The contrary, as any reader of him knows, is true. In all the world there is no more feeling poet. He proves it in a hundred ways, no one of which is logically defensible; has he not demonstrated, even to monotony, the foolishness of tears? It is now that the great poet emerges, the poet whose humanity is profounder than his thought. He is that most moving kind of man, the kind that tries not to feel yet does; he is that most convincing of lovers, the one who begins by thinking he does not believe in love. Hardy should scorn the emotions of himself and others; instead of which, he lets them break his heart.

The intensity of his concern may show itself in bizarre, unlikely ways, but there is no mistaking the intensity, as for example in "The Head Above the Fog," which gives life to a mistress in the very act of decapitating her:

> Something do I see
> Above the fog that sheets the mead,
> A figure like to life indeed,
> Moving along with spectre-speed,
>   Seen by none but me.
>
> O the vision keen!—

Tripping along to me for love
As in the flesh it used to move,
Only its hat and plume above
   The evening fog-fleece seen.

  In the day-fall wan,
When nighted birds break off their song,
Mere ghostly head it skims along,
Just as it did when warm and strong,
   Body seeming gone.

  Such it is I see
Above the fog that sheets the mead—
Yea, that which once could breathe and plead!—
Skimming along with spectre-speed
   To a last tryst with me.

The intensity in this case is not Hardy's, it is the ghost's, and the skimming speed of the ghost is what conveys it to us. Hardy is never without the power, indispensable in any ambitious poet, to endow his creations with an energy that seems to be their own. It is he who speaks, but it is they who have the final word. "The Head Above the Fog" treats of a tryst: a favorite subject with Hardy, for nothing interests him more than meetings between lovers; the most moving number for him is two. The meetings are more often sad than successful, but no matter; his deepest sympathies are engaged, and there is always something beautiful in that depth. He may or may not be recording a personal experience; most of the time, he tells us in his prefaces, he is not. It is clear enough that twenty-one poems in *Satires of Circumstance* have to do with the death of his first wife, with whom he had lived thirty-eight years; and these poems are not to be matched in all the literature of grief. Usually, however, we are willing to assume that he is dramatic, or as he himself liked to say, "personative." Whether or not the rule applies to the

poem *Near Lanivet, 1872*, we could no more take it for unreal
than we could so take *Othello* or *King Lear*.

> There was a stunted handpost just on the crest,
>   Only a few feet high:
> She was tired, and we stopped in the twilight-time
>   for her rest,
>   At the crossroads close thereby.
>
> She leant back, being so weary, against its stem,
>   And laid her arms on its own,
> Each open palm stretched out to each end of them,
>   Her sad face sideways thrown.
>
> Her white-clothed form at this dim-lit cease of day
>   Made her look as one crucified
> In my gaze at her from the midst of the dusty way,
>   And hurriedly "Don't," I cried.
>
> I do not think she heard. Loosing thence she said,
>   As she stepped forth ready to go,
> "I am rested now.—Something strange came into my head;
>   I wish I had not leant so!"
>
> And wordless we moved onward down from the hill
>   In the west cloud's murked obscure,
> And looking back we could see the handpost still
>   In the solitude of the moor.
>
> "It struck her too," I thought, for as if afraid
>   She heavily breathed as we trailed;
> Till she said, "I did not think how 'twould look in
>   the shade,
>   When I leant there like one nailed."
>
> I, lightly: "There's nothing in it. For *you*, anyhow!"
>   —"O I know there is not," said she . . .
> "Yet I wonder. . . . If no one is bodily crucified now,
>   In spirit one may be!"

> And we dragged on and on, while we seemed to see
>   In the running of Time's far glass
> Her crucified, as she had wondered if she might be
>   Some day.—Alas, alas!

His lovers are sometimes faithful, sometimes faithless; though as often as not the faithless onces are merely feeble of purpose, perhaps for a reason they cannot understand—they change, and are bewildered by the change. If they are cruel, it may be unintentionally so, or else they remain unaware that they were cruel. "A Maiden's Pledge" is the song of an absolutely faithful girl who will continue so even if her lover never hints of marriage:

> Your comet-comings I will wait
> With patience time shall not wear through.

Hardy takes pleasure in that, as in one of his best-known songs, "Let Me Enjoy," he says he takes pleasure in countless sweet things that are not for him.

> Let me enjoy the earth no less
> Because the all-enacting Might
> That fashioned forth its loveliness
> Had other aims than my delight. . . .
>
> From manuscripts of moving song
> Inspired by scenes and dreams unknown,
> I'll pour out raptures that belong
> To others, as they were my own.

His singular devotion to birds—one could almost say, his obsession with them—has something like this for its source. The intensity of birds, equal to his own, caught him up in their ecstasies as they sang or sported; or suffered, for he had no defenses against the spectacle of one in pain, particularly such a one as he addresses in " The Blinded Bird." His rage against men who run red-hot needles through the eyes of songbirds to increase the sweetness of their voices is stated only by indirection, yet the rage is strong enough:

> Who hath charity? This bird.
> Who suffereth long and is kind,
> Is not provoked, though blind
> And alive ensepulchred?
> Who hopeth, endureth all things?
> Who thinketh no evil, but sings?
> Who is divine? This bird.

For Hardy, it would seem, birds were omens: they had been sent to tell him something. In " The Darkling Thrush " the message is that hope may have some meaning after all, for this bird if not for him. But another thrush, seen out of his window on Christmas day, told him something else again:

> There, to reach a rotting berry,
> Toils a thrush,—constrained to very
> Dregs of food by sharp distress,
> Taking such with thankfulness.

> Why, O starving bird, when I
> One day's joy would justify,
> And put misery out of view,
> Did you make me notice you?

Hardy never ceases to take testimony, to read the world as if it were a book, now closed, now open, with too many pages in it ever to let him finish. A tree in London can strike pity out of him because it is not in the country where it belongs. But sometimes it is he who is being read, as in the case of the fallow deer that looked in upon him one night:

We do not discern those eyes
　　Watching in the snow;
Lit by lamps of rosy dyes
We do not discern those eyes
　　Wondering, aglow,
　　Fourfooted, tiptoe.

A poet's power to feel is best proved in the stories he tells, provided he can tell stories. Hardy could; that was where his genius lay; and so it may be that the heart of the *Collected Poems* beats in the narratives that throng it like so many persons, each one of them powerful in his or her own right. The final richness, perhaps, is here. Hardy is the envy of those who would be infinitely fertile in narrative ideas if only they could; it would seem to have been easy for him to be just that. Doubtless he worked harder than appears; there is evidence that he scoured newspapers for material, and took copious notes on stories he overheard in his native Wessex. The appearance, nevertheless, is of a fountain that cannot stop flowing; and its waters are strong waters that thrust forth from deep places. Hardy's stories are little melodramas, sensational, unrelenting, and if need be mournful beyond bearing, as the great ballads are.

In "The Burghers" a man who has planned to ambush his wife and her lover—to kill them with two strokes of his sword as they flee from his house—brings them home with him instead and heaps gifts upon them, of clothes and jewels; then he lets them go, knowing that his kindness to them is a wound which will never heal. In "Her Death and After" a dying wife tells her former lover that she wishes the child she has just borne were his; her husband is not kind to her, and she fears for the child's future, for it is lame. The lover haunts her tomb until it becomes noticeable that he does; the husband himself notices it, and comes to ask him why; then without premeditation he tells the husband that the lame child is his. The child is sent to him and he brings it up, happily because this is what the dead woman would have wished, unhappily because he has hurt her name.

In "The Dance at the Phoenix" a woman of sixty who in her youth had been free with her favors, especially to "sundry troopers of the King's Own Cavalry," is now the virtuous wife of a gentle fellow who knows nothing of this past; and she would have died peacefully in good time had not on a certain evening the King's Cavalry come to the Phoenix Inn for a dance like those of the old days. Jenny, sleeping by her husband, hears the music and cannot refrain from slipping away to join the merriment, old as she is. She dances all night; is escorted home; slips back into bed; and dies of exhaustion which her husband attributes to some natural cause—"The King's said not a word." In "A Sunday Morning Tragedy" a mother tells how, having failed to persuade her daughter's lover that he should marry her because she is with child by him, procures from an herb woman a drug that will dispose of the child; only after she has administered the drug does she hear that the lover, repenting, has published the banns in church; but it is too late, for the drug proves fatal to the daughter. In "The Noble Lady's Tale" the lady's husband, an actor who has given up the stage to please her father, begs her for permission to go back and play for just one night; she consents; he goes, but when he is home again he accuses her of having followed him to the theater, nor does he believe her oaths to the contrary; he finally decides that her wraith had followed him rather than herself in flesh and blood; but this distresses him quite as much, since it suggests that she had not trusted him; he wastes away, and so does she, unable to be sure whether a projection of her had pursued him; yet those who listen to her tale are left with further questions:

> Did she, we wonder, follow
> Jealously?
> And were those protests hollow?—
> Or saw he
> Some semblant dame? Or can wraiths really be?

In " The Moth-Signal " a woman, sitting with her husband one night, tells him she pities a moth that is burning in the candle flame; she goes outdoors to see how the weather is, and her lover comes to her from a tumulus nearby; he remarks that the moth she put out of the window is " burnt and broken," as he is, for he has shattered his own marriage vows; and an ancient Briton speaks from the tumulus, saying people are what they used to be. In " The Sacrilege " a woman of the roads promises her lover that she will go no more to meet his rival, Wrestler Joe, provided he will steal treasure from the cathedral shrine with which she can buy ear-drops and rings; the lover sets off to do this, but only after engaging his brother to murder her in the event that the theft is traced to him (whereupon he will be hanged) and she then takes up with Wrestler Joe; things do go that way, and the brother drowns the woman, whose screams as she dies he will never cease to hear.

In a companion story, " A Trampwoman's Tragedy," the heroine pretends, for no reason she can understand in the sequel, that the child she carries is the child not of her " fancy-man " but of " Jeering John," his rival. Her fancy-man stabs Jeering John to death; is hanged; and leaves the woman wondering why she had done such a mad thing; her only comfort being that she can reassure the ghost of her lover whenever it appears and pleads to be told the truth. In " The Statue of Liberty " a man is asked why he scrubs with mop and water the statue that stands in a city square; his answer is not that he is paid by the city guardians to do it, or that he loves liberty, which the statue symbolizes; it is simply that his daughter was the sculptor's model, and that she had died in this city, distant from his, before he could visit her; what he does now is the only favor he can do his darling, whose good name he thus preserves; but he does not know that he is speaking to the sculptor himself, and that the sculptor knows what happened to the daughter—she died " in the dens of vice." And so on. The list seems to be endless, for Hardy's narrative vein never runs out.

Now and then there is a hearty, humorous tale, since Hardy had that in him too: "The Bride-Night Fire," or "The Home-coming," the latter with a fine refrain:

> Gruffly growled the wind on Toller downland broad and bare,
> And lonesome was the house, and dark; and few came there.

But the prevailing tone is sombre, and the accidents of love or hate, of innocence or guilt, are lighted by an artist in the wings who knows everything about shades and shadows.

He knows everything about time as well. Not only do his stories happen, as all stories do, in time; time is also his very subject. No poet has known better how to move forward and backward in this strangest of dimensions. The poem "One We Knew" concerns an old woman whose memories were pictures for others to study as well as herself:

> She said she had often heard the gibbet creaking
>   As it swayed in the lightning flash,
> Had caught from the neighboring town a small child's shrieking
>   At the cart-tail under the lash. . . .
>
> With cap-framed face and long gaze into the embers—
>   We seated around her knees—

She would dwell on such dead themes, not as one who remembers,
But as one who sees.

She resembled Hardy in that, for his own memories were like
things printed on a wall; anything that had happened to him,
or had happened to his imagination, was real as present things
were unable to be. He lived in his own gallery of paintings;
nor could he be sure how many of the figures there were ghosts.
This philosopher who prided himself upon his hardness of mind
saw ghosts; he had no business to, but he did. They were the
spirits of murdered persons, or of persons otherwise wronged; but
then too they could be of the mildest sort, like those in "The
Garden Seat":

> At night when reddest flowers are black
> Those who once sat thereon come back;
> Quite a row of them sitting there,
> Quite a row of them sitting there.
>
> With them the seat does not break down,
> Nor winter freeze them, nor floods drown,
> For they are light as upper air,
> They are as light as upper air!

Perhaps the most touching of them all is in the tale of the dead
sailor's mother who comes nightly to the house where she used
to live and waits for her son to appear; it is the only house he
remembers, and so is the only one he can haunt.

Old houses interest anybody, but for Hardy they were tombs
in which time was buried. But buried as it were alive, so that it
moved there, and even spoke or sang there, like one of his
authentic ghosts. An old mirror, he assumed, must be haunted
by the images that had been made upon it; one of his poems,
"The Cheval-Glass," tells of a man who bought at an auction
the mirror before which a woman he once had loved stood

nightly and brushed her hair; he said he saw her in it still, and would keep it with him till he died. Old furniture must remember, Hardy thought, the people who had used it; indeed it must reflect them:

> Hands upon hands, growing paler and paler,
>   As in a mirror a candle-flame
> Shows images of itself, each frailer
>   As it recedes, though the eye may frame
>   Its shape the same.

There was not too much difference for Hardy between an old English house and a prehistoric tumulus or barrow, or a Roman ruin: those had been houses too, if only for bones. The bones still slept there; they even dreamed, and he could hear them talking in their sleep. But the official antiquities of his island were really no older for him than things he himself had seen or done long years ago. Time, that relative thing, was so relative in his case that a certain Roman road on which as a child he had walked with his mother was ancient to him rather for that reason than for the reason that helmed legionaries once marched along it. His imagination had always a temporal cast. His genius could endow things with age that had none otherwise, just as it could read into a single moment, recollected and reconsidered, eternities of meaning which as it passed had not been recognized; the present moment, he is always saying, contains all time and more, but nobody knows this then. Railway trains and stations, for all their bleakness, which he never minimizes, take on in his poems the dignity of timeless crossroads where anything on earth can happen, or anything in hell or heaven.

His love of music is chiefly the love of country singing—old singing, of songs and hymns not much remembered now. His poems ring with the quaint names of former tunes, just as they shake with the feet of dancers: not merely her of the Phoenix Inn, but countless young and old performers of forgotten steps. Church choirs, and groups of warblers by night, serenading bridegrooms or celebrating births and deaths—these have a peculiar, almost a sacred importance for Hardy, who knows the names of ancient instruments, too, and is learned in the folklore of bells. One of his best stories, " The Chapel-Organist," deals with a woman who would rather die than cease to play

> Old Hundredth, Saint Stephen's,
> Mount Zion, New Sabbath, Miles-Lane, Holy Rest, and Arabia, and Eaton.

And the whole subject comes perfectly into focus as he watches some young girls in a winter street singing songs whose origins are venerable beyond their comprehension:

> Yea, old notes like those
> Here are living on yet!—
> But of their fame and fashion
> How little these know
> Who strum without passion
> For pence in the snow!

Hardy hugged time to himself as he hugged pain and gloom; they were the three dimensions of his universe, in which he felt so much at home that he could be surprised when readers complained of its barrenness. It was thick and warm for him, like an old coat that exactly fitted him, even if it looked a little long, and indeed drooped to the ground. It was what he recognized as reality, the one thing to which he was entirely committed. The bitterness of the world did not forbid him to embrace it: a poor thing, but his own. At times, to be sure, he wondered whether he missed something that others saw; he peered hard, and had the reward of any pessimist—something was better than he expected. For that matter, many things were; even all things, if one did not mind their being just what they were. Now and then he would offer an apology for the low tones in which he spoke: he but sang his part, as others must sing theirs. There is in fact much kindness in him, a sort of subdued good nature which shines through his frown as well as his smile; for he smiled and was humorous, too, he had a nice sense of the absurd. He was susceptible to superstitions for which his philosophy would have had no use. Oxen *might* kneel on Christmas Eve; and of course there were all those ghosts; there was true love, too, a thing that mechanism would not explain.

His mind was complicated, and so was his art. The effect of plainness in his poems can make us overlook their skill: a conscious thing with him, and the product of study. He seems to be interested in nothing but accuracy of statement, even if this means that he must sometimes sound clumsy and crude; exactness is what he wants, and he will sacrifice everything to it. This is true; and it is true of any great poet; there is nothing else that causes us in the end to love poetry at all. But accuracy is itself an art, a fine and high one which all the muses conspire to praise. Hardy's muses, he said in 1887, were five in number: Form, Tune, Story, Dance, and Hymn. The last of these may surprise us a little until we read him through again and realize how often he was lyric in the rich, free, leaping way of the Elizabethans:

> This is the weather the cuckoo likes,
>   And so do I;
> When showers betumble the chestnut spikes,
>   And nestlings fly:

> And the little brown nightingale bills his best,
> And they sit outside at " The Travellers' Rest,"
> And maids come forth sprig-muslin drest,
> And citizens dream of the south and west,
>   And so do I.

Or until we remember how various his stanzas are; he studied the stanza like a musician, and made it his idiom, whether intricate as in " The Discovery ":

> I wandered to a crude coast
>   Like a ghost;
> Upon the hills I saw fires—
>   Funeral pyres
> Seemingly—and heard breaking
> Waves like distant cannonades that set the land shaking;

or simple as in " The Pine Planters (Marty South's Reverie) ":

> We work here together
>   In blast and breeze;
> He fills the earth in,
>   I hold the trees.
>
> He does not notice
>   That what I do
> Keeps me from moving
>   And chills me through . . .
>
> I have helped him so many,
>   So many days,
> But never win any
>   Small word of praise!

Hardy was a musician; he was also an etcher. It was not for nothing that he had practiced architecture; the draughtsman in him is always coming out. He has the keen eye that feeling cannot confuse—an old man's eye, we are tempted to say, which

misses nothing. Some of his poems are pure studies in black and
white of things he saw in passing: " An East-End Curate," for
example, or " No Buyers: A Street Scene," or " Nobody Comes."
Others are masterpieces with weather for their theme: any kind
of weather, for Hardy liked it all, but his specialty was rain, as in
" A Sheep Fair ":

> The day arrives of the autumn fair,
>   And torrents fall,
> Though sheep in throngs are gathered there,
>   Ten thousand all,
> Sodden, with hurdles round them reared:
> And, lot by lot, the pens are cleared,
> And the auctioneer wrings out his beard,
> And wipes his book, bedrenched and smeared,
> And rakes the rain from his face with the edge of his hand,
>   As torrents fall.
>
> The wool of the ewes is like a sponge
>   With the daylong rain:
> Jammed tight, to turn, or lie, or lunge,
>   They strive in vain.
> Their horns are soft as finger-nails,
> Their shepherds reek against the rails,
> The tied dogs soak with tucked-in tails,
> The buyers' hat-brims fill like pails,
> Which spill small cascades when they shift their stand
>   In the daylong rain.

Not that these particular sheep were before him as he wrote;
a third stanza of the poem says it was long ago that he went
to Pummery Fair, " and the hoarse auctioneer is dead." But
time had not faded the impression—time, the sixth muse of
Thomas Hardy.

The world of the *Collected Poems* is a great world. It is *the*
great world, seen always as Hardy saw it, with quizzical, deep

eyes that both formed and deformed it. But the deformation was no crime; it was rather a style, a way of twisting things into the shape his genius saw. This is often a queer shape. What other poet, wishing to tell his beloved that he would be hers even in the grave, ever expressed the hope

That thy worm should be my worm, Love?

Worms were as much his specialty as weather.

The leaf drops: earthworms draw it in
At night-time noiselessly.

That is a small event among the many that take place in the great world. But Hardy noticed it, and having noticed it he must put it down. Of the several epitaphs he composed for himself, none is more simple and true than "Afterwards," with this refrain to be spoken by his neighbors:

"He was a man who used to notice such things."

Index

Apollonius, 18
Aquinas, St. Thomas, 12, 28
Aristarchus, 18
Aristotle, 11, 17
Arnold, M., 49
Auden, W. H., 15
Augustine, St., 39

Baudelaire, C. P., 39, 75
Blake, W., 80
Brooke, L., 77
Brooks, C., 45
Browne, T., 80
Browning, R., 7
Bruno, G., 11
Burnet, T., 79
Burns, R., 32

Caedmon, 14
Churchill, C., 71
Copernicus, N., 20
Croce, B., 15, 25-6, 40

Dante, 11-12, 20, 28-9, 39
Darwin, C., 33
Democritus, 10
De Quincey, T., 79
Dickinson, E., 38, 75
Dio Cassius, 3
Donne, J., 32, 44-8, 51, 56-8, 60-1,
    68, 72, 80
Dostoevsky, F. M., 37
Drayton, M., 22
Dryden, J., 67

Eliot, T. S., 46, 81
Elizabeth I, 52
Empedocles, 10-11
Epicurus, 12
Euclid, 13
Euripides, 6, 17
Eustathius, 18

Fichte, J. G., 11
Frost, R., 81

Frye, N., 32

Galileo, G., 20
Gascoigne, G., 45, 49, 60–1, 69
Geoffrey of Monmouth, 5, 7
Greville, F., 45, 51, 58, 61, 69
Guarini, G., 21

Hall, J. C., 42
Hardy, T., 83–107
Heraclitus, 10
Herbert, G., 32
Herrick, R., 80
Hobbes, T., 71
Homer, 17–18, 20, 30, 35
Hopkins, G. M., 15
Hotson, L., 53–5

James I, 52–3
Jonson, B., 45–6, 48–9, 51, 58, 60–2,
    67–9, 72, 74, 77

Keats, J., 36
Kepler, J., 20
Kermode, F., 71

Leconte de Lisle, C. M. R., 75
Locke, J., 71
Lucian, 3–4
Lucretius, 11

Mallarmé, S., 55, 71
Manilius, 18
Marlowe, C., 22
Marvell, A., 32, 44, 47
McBride, H., 79
Metrodorus, 18
Milton, J., 8, 10, 14, 20, 32
Montaigne, M., 2
Muir, E., 24–43

Napoleon, 85

Nashe, T., 61
Newton, I., 20

Ovid, 35

Pascal, B., 83
Paul, St., 76
Peterson, D., 57
Pindar, 18
Plato, 2, 10, 39, 70
Plotinus, 21
Pope, A., 16, 26, 67, 78
Porter, K. A., 78
Pound, E., 26, 71, 74
Ptolemy, 20

Raleigh, W., 45, 49, 60, 69
Ransom, J. C., 47
Rollins, H., 52

Santayana, G., 11
Scaliger, J. C., 21
Schiller, F., 15
Schopenhauer, A., 11
Shakespeare, W., 5–7, 10, 13, 20–2,
    32, 47–55, 58, 60, 62, 68, 72, 74
Shelley, P. B., 10
Sidney, P., 2, 10, 20, 45, 60–1, 69,
    72
Sitwell, E., 76–82
Sitwell, G., 79
Smart, C., 80
Socrates, 10
Southampton, Earl of, 52–3
Spender, S., 42
Spenser, E., 45
Stevens, W., 57, 72, 74–5

Tasso, T., 22
Theagenes, 18
Thomas, D., 80
Thucydides, 2–3

Tolstoy, 85
Traherne, T., 15–16, 32
Tuckerman, F. G., 75

Valéry, P., 38, 72, 75, 81
Vaughan, H., 44
Vico, G. B., 15

Virgil, 25, 40

Williams, W. C., 77
Wilson, T., 57
Wordsworth, W., 7, 15, 41
Wyatt, T., 45, 69

Yeats, W. B., 82